T0302481

Advance Praise for
CHANGING THE CORPORATE LANDSCAPE

"Jean Otte has planted a grand seed of possibility for leaders who truly embrace the privilege of nurturing the flowering talents around them. This is a book to be both read and treasured."

—Robert J. Danzig, author, *The Leader Within You;* former CEO, the Hearst Newspaper Group

"Jean Otte, creator and leader of one of the most innovative personal development programs for women, provides unique insight into the challenges women face in succeeding in the corporate world—her personal experiences, learnings gained from ten years of WOMEN Unlimited Inc. and her garden metaphors make for a read that forces you to think and take action."

—Lois Juliber, COO, Colgate

"Jean Otte offers pragmatic and effective advice about how to change the corporate landscape based on learnings from her personal experiences as a corporate leader and from ten years of work with her highly successful WOMEN Unlimited Inc. programs. Jean has a lot to teach us about how to nurture and grow women leaders."

—Marcia Brumit Kropf, Ph.D., COO, Girls Incorporated

"Jean Otte has an unbelievable passion for helping women excel in the corporate world. Our company is fortunate to have had a number of our female executives participate in Jean's WOMEN Unlimited Inc. leadership programs. I was also able to attend one of the sessions and I experienced, firsthand, why the programs are so successful. This book is another extension of that success."

—John Lampe, CEO & president, Bridgestone Americas Holding Inc.

"Jean Otte speaks directly to every woman in corporate life who ever wondered 'what do you have to do to get ahead around here, anyway?' She knows what she's talking about, her advice has been tested on real women doing real jobs, and she has a delicious sense of humor that helps keep even the hard stuff from feeling overwhelming."

—Ronna Lichtenberg, author, *It's Not Business, It's Personal*

"*Changing the Corporate Landscape* is a road map to corporate leadership that draws on the experiences of the women who have successfully traveled these roads before. It is for every woman who wants to adeptly navigate around the roadblocks they face on their way to the top."

—Lee E. Miller, coauthor,
A Woman's Guide to Successful Negotiating: How to Convince, Collaborate, and Create Your Way to Agreement

"Jean Otte has a refreshing, insightful view of leadership development, drawn from her wealth of experience working with participants in WOMEN Unlimited Inc. programs around the United States. Her garden metaphor provides a vibrant, tangible frame of reference for leaders, new and mature, striving to motivate and engage their employees in the high pressure, 24/7 world of the 21st century."

—Rennie Roberts, executive director & CEO, YWCA of the City of New York, former head of human resources, American Express Company

"This down-to-earth guide provides women with an opportunity to reflect on the realities of the workplace and illustrates real-life examples of how women are leading and succeeding."

—Leonora Valvo, president, Global Executive

"Jean Otte's vision, intellect, and sense of humor have stirred corporate America to take notice of the rocky road women still travel. She has provided strong road maps leaders can follow to pave the way for women's advancement. Jean inspires women to be bold, powerful, and courageous. Her formula challenges women to see how they can sabotage their own success, and she provides practical tools to help them remove these obstacles to achieving greatness."

—Claudette Whiting, senior diversity director, Microsoft

CHANGING THE CORPORATE LANDSCAPE

CHANGING THE CORPORATE LANDSCAPE

A woman's guide to cultivating leadership excellence

JEAN written by OTTE

LONGSTREET PRESS
Atlanta, Georgia

WWW.LONGSTREETPRESS.NET

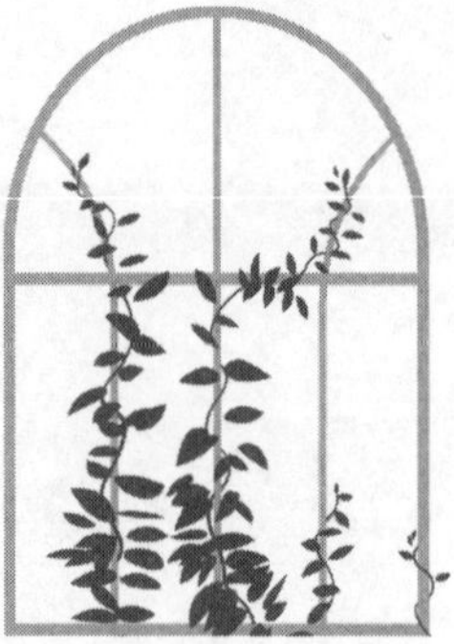

Published by
Longstreet Press, Inc.
2974 Hardman Court
Atlanta, Georgia 30305

Copyright © 2004 by Jean Otte

All rights reserved. No part of this book may be reproduced in any form or by any means without the prior written permission of the Publisher, excepting brief quotations used in connection with review, written specifically for inclusion in a magazine or newspaper.

Printed in the United States of America

First printing: April 2004
1 3 5 7 9 10 8 6 4 2

ISBN: 1-56352-735-9
Library of Congress Control Number: 2004103758

Jacket design and illustrations by Subset Design • Ithinand Tubkam
Book interior design by Tammy S. Grimes
www.tsgcrescent.com• tsgcrescent@charter.net

For my family and cherished friends, whose love
and support continues to help me bloom and grow

Acknowledgments

If you have ever gazed at a truly beautiful garden, admiring its wide variety of flowers and plants, you know how difficult it is to select one or two when asked to name the greatest contributors to the garden's beauty. Each plant has a specific role in creating that beauty. When attempting to acknowledge and thank all of the wonderful, unique, and special people in my "garden," I truly appreciate the many prized individuals who collectively have made a difference in my life, and continue to enrich it every day.

One of my refrigerator magnets has the following anonymous quote written on it: "The most beautiful flower in life's garden is a friend." To all of you (and you do know who you are!), I offer my sincere appreciation for your support, encouragement, and contributions in the writing of this book. I am truly blessed to have such a glorious garden of friends.

This book could not have been written without the support of all the WUI corporate partners, the managers, mentors, and thousands of women nationwide who have participated and shared their expertise in the WUI leadership development programs during the past 10 years. A sincere thank-you to all of you for your commitment to the continuing growth and development of your leadership excellence and for helping to make a difference in the lives of so many!

I also acknowledge and thank all of the past colleagues and managers with whom I worked in corporate America for over 30 years. The knowledge I gained as part of that benchmarking experience has served to help me progress in my career and, most important, to enable me to share that experience with so many others seeking to grow and develop their leadership skills.

One final note of appreciation goes to my editor, Callie Rucker Oettinger. Callie worked tirelessly with me to make my vision of this book a reality, even when she was in the midst of producing her own great work—her son, Max, who arrived within a month of *Changing the Corporate Landscape's* deadline. Thank you, Callie! I look forward to your becoming one of the perennials in my garden!

CONTENTS

FOREWORD

Ten years ago, Jean Otte founded WOMEN Unlimited. Since then, she has worked with thousands of women throughout corporate America, helping them develop their potential as individuals and as leaders. *Changing the Corporate Landscape* is a "best of" Jean. It is a combination of two of her passions—her love of gardens and for helping women to succeed in business.

"Success is gender neutral" is a phrase that Jean has repeated hundreds of times over the years. *Changing the Corporate Landscape* explores the tools necessary for women to cultivate success. Drawing a parallel between gardening and business practices, Jean shares the achievements and advice of some of today's most-respected business leaders. Jean also pulls from her own 30+ years of experience in the corporate world, as well as the experiences of the thousands of women who have participated in her organization's unique leadership development programs, to explore the best and worst leadership practices.

Jean's insightful and often humorous "Thottes" (Otte's thoughts) touch on such topics as helping people "bloom and grow," office pest control, weeding and pruning, creating high-growth environments, and assessing the garden shed for the tools to success.

"You cannot light another's path without brightening your own" is another phrase Jean often repeats. Although she cannot tell you where she first heard this quote, she can tell you the role it has played in her work. Leaders who mentor others continue to develop themselves. They gain perspective and growth.

In the garden, a leader may be a trellis, supporting an employee. The leader offers the structure helping the employee achieve new heights. At the same time, the leader benefits from the growth and beauty the employee adds to the garden. This cyclical model of achieving success by promoting strategic alliance between employees and leaders, to benefit the individuals and ultimately the organizations for which they work, is a key theme in *Changing the Corporate Landscape.*

Although *Changing the Corporate Landscape* was clearly written for women in the workplace, it offers numerous examples that both men and women will find helpful.

GAIL EVANS
former executive vice president of CNN;
author, *Play Like a Man, Win Like a Woman*
and *She Wins, You Win*

FOREWORD

Leadership in today's world is many things. It is creating and sharing a vision for an organization—a vision that takes it to a better, more successful place. Equally important, it is motivating people to achieve that vision. It is leading by example. It is aggressively pursuing enhanced performance and higher results. At the same time, leadership is displaying and emphasizing integrity—at all times, without compromise. It is displaying and exemplifying a positive, can-do attitude, combining perseverance, agility, and the will to succeed. And, most important, leadership is about recognizing that all we do, we do through people.

Every successful company knows its only truly sustainable competitive advantage is its people. Products or services can be copied. It is the people—the employees—that truly differentiate a company. Some view attention to people as the "soft stuff," but those truly in the know recognize that the soft stuff *is* the hard stuff. It is through people that we conduct our business, and through people that we must focus to improve our business's performance. The strongest workforce is the one that has the broadest array of talent—that is, the biggest variety of competencies and skills. And the smartest and easiest way to that end is to diversify the workforce. A company's employee base should reflect its customer base and society at large. When we think about diversity and mirroring the world we live in, gender is clearly the first focus of attention. With some 51% of the world's population being women, it goes without saying that a representative level of women in an organization, namely its proportionate share of the female population in the workplace, is a desirable thing.

In the many positions I have held at KeySpan, I have been motivated to support my fellow employees and do all I can to support their growth. As a result, I have mentored, hired, and promoted women into traditionally male-dominated positions in my industry, and championed their growth. Women bring all of the attributes of leadership cited above, and in addition, they bring another dimension to the human quality of management. Women can bring another perspective on emotional intelligence, on employee relations, on consideration and interaction, to the workplace. Just as humankind has celebrated the differences and the complementary blending of man and woman since the beginning of time, so can business today. It is all part of KeySpan's commitment to the value of diversity in every sense of the term. Focusing on diversity as a corporate value makes us a stronger, more talented, company and one that is much more capable of responding to our diverse customer base.

Smart, strong, and solid businesspeople today recognize the inherent value in a workplace that is balanced from a gender perspective. They see value, and welcome such diversity and support it. Being supportive means providing a work environment in which all individuals feel recognized, respected, and supported, regardless of what makes up that individuality. It means providing opportunities for people to perform, providing personal guidance and support, and standing side by side with fellow employees as they try to succeed.

One of the actions I look back on with pride is bringing the WOMEN Unlimited organization into KeySpan. My first exposure to the program, at the recommendation of one of our board members, was to meet Jean Otte and hear firsthand about this wonderful organization and Jean's pioneering efforts in founding it. Since then, Jean has grown the organization to one of stature and respect, to one clearly recognizable for what it can do to develop women. It has become one of the organizations that smart, savvy, and results-oriented companies want to be part of. As a result of those early meetings, KeySpan signed on a few of our high-potential women, and I became a mentor. In short order we realized this was an opportunity to provide an excellent developmental experience not only for our women employees but also for our men and women who participated as mentors.

In WOMEN Unlimited, as in this book, Jean Otte demonstrates how women can be motivated, developed, and enriched in today's society. She excels in her ability to develop confidence and leadership and—bottom line—the ability to perform and achieve results. Readers will find this book inspirational and rewarding, just as participants find the WOMEN Unlimited program.

For those of you who think you've mastered the art of supporting women, I encourage you to read on and learn more. As Will Rogers once said: "Even if you're on the right track, you'll get run over if you just sit there."

I am proud and fortunate to hold Jean Otte as a business colleague and a friend. All those she touches are better off for knowing her. Read this book, absorb its teachings and insights, practice its advice, and watch your company excel. When all is said and done, it's not the best man for the job, or the best woman, it's the best person—give them all a fair chance!

WALLACE P. PARKER, JR.
president, KeySpan Corporation

Introduction

> *"We are stardust*
> *We are golden*
> *And we've got to get ourselves*
> *Back to the garden."*
> *—Joni Mitchell*

Changing the Corporate Landscape offers real-life examples and suggestions to serve as a woman's guide to achieving greater success in the workplace. In this book I share the key learnings from my own work experiences, including the highlights and lowlights, and, most important, the experiences of thousands of participants, managers, facilitators, and mentors who have participated in WOMEN Unlimited Inc.'s (WUI) nationwide, cross-industry leadership development programs. Including input from respected colleagues, and reflections on and from past leaders, this book is intended to serve as a guide for both those who want to develop their leadership knowledge and skills and those who have the desire to facilitate the development of others.

I drew my inspiration for *Changing the Corporate Landscape* from my early love of gardens. I was born in Essex, England, just before the start of WWII. We British are famous gardeners. We love to talk about our gardens. In fact, much of the conversation in England—when it is not about the weather—is about gardening. It is a source of national pride. Since food rationing continued for many years after the war, gardening became particularly important because it was a source of food. My father had a beautiful flower garden, a large vegetable garden, and a "victory garden," in which he planted additional vegetables. I spent a lot of time helping my father with the gardens, watching him and listening as he explained the differences between growing different types of vegetables and flowers.

I remember being frustrated with my little patch of soil when I was a child. The seeds I planted never seemed to grow. I remember going to the garden with my father one day, thinking it was all a waste of time—until I saw my plants peeking through the soil for the first time. I felt such a thrill and a wonderful feeling of satisfaction and pride when they finally bloomed. Some seeds, like some people, take longer to sprout. There is certainly a lot of unseen growth occurring belowground, but it can take some plants a while to appear aboveground. During a trip to Japan a few years back, I listened to the owner of a large hotel chain discuss the process of convincing organizations to embrace and take on the process of improvement. He compared it to bamboo, discussing how it takes bamboo many years to break the surface from its seedling stage. It can be very disappointing and frustrating for people who do not understand the growth pattern of bamboo or do not have the patience to wait. However, once bamboo surfaces, it grows incredibly fast in a short period of time—sometimes six to ten feet.

In both my business and personal life, I have drawn a parallel between gardening and human development. There was no doubt in my mind that principles used to develop and understand the growth of plants could be used with people. For example, most seeds cannot simply be thrown into a garden and expected to grow on their own. Some seeds will grow only in certain soils. Some need sun, while others need shade, to sprout. Like people, they need to be planted in the right place and nurtured.

I observed in myself and many others how important it is to be in a workplace environment where one's interests and abilities match the job requirements. Years ago I was asked to take on an employee from the accounts payable/receivable area. The employee was not doing well, but he was bright and his manager did not want to fire him. On his first day in my customer service area, I asked him about his previous job and what he most liked and disliked about it. His response was: "I hate working with numbers. I was never good at math in school and I'm always afraid I'm going to make a big mistake." The story has a happy ending. He became a superstar in the customer service area. His personality and interpersonal skills were exactly what we needed. He received praise from customers and work colleagues, and later became one of the company's top outside sales representatives. As I learned in my garden, sometimes growth is simply a matter of environment.

For many years I had a dream tucked away in my head—an idea for creating an organization specifically to help women advance in the corporate world. After over 30 years of corporate experience, including being the first female executive and officer at National Car Rental (NCR), I was ready for a change. At this point, a series of life-altering events occurred that resulted in my following what I knew was my passion.

Within a four-month span, both my husband and mother died; my eldest son graduated from college, married, and moved away; my younger son joined the Marines and was sent overseas to Operation Desert Storm; and NCR was about to be sold again. All these events led me to rethink what I wanted to do with my life. I began reflecting and reassessing what really mattered to me. How did I want to move forward? Did I want to stay with NCR and try to align myself with the new corporate executives? Did I want to go to another corporation and do something similar there? The more I thought about it, the more I began to see that my true satisfaction and passion came from helping to develop the leadership potential of others. I realized that my entrepreneurial spirit was ready to explore the myriad of opportunities I believed intuitively were out there. The idea of starting my own business and becoming my own boss excited me. I knew I would have a far greater sense of fulfillment and satisfaction if I could design and operate my own business. The more I thought about this exciting opportunity, the more I realized my true passion would be far better served if I used my abilities and the lessons I had learned to help women develop into leaders.

One of my personal heroes, author John Gardner, wrote: "All too often we're giving people cut flowers, when we should be teaching them to grow their own plants." When I launched WUI, it was rooted in the purpose of helping women facilitate their own growth. Ten years later, from that small seed, WUI has become a nationwide organization that continues to bring together women who truly want to achieve more in their professional and personal lives. It is not a "fix-it" program for women who do not have the desire to achieve higher goals. Unlike the typical training sessions professionals attend, during which they learn from a presenter, WUI draws knowledge from the participants rather than bring knowledge to them. WUI creates an environment in which subject matter is presented and direction offered, with the participants leading the session. The programs help participants nurture their ideas and express their concerns, issues, and thoughts. They also have participants work together to get the most out of a particular subject. And, most significant, they learn how to apply it to their own lives. WUI operates on the premise that everyone who attends its programs has something unique to contribute, from which others can learn. As I have watched women "bloom and grow" in business, I feel just as I did as a child when I saw those very first flowers bloom.

When looking back over my journals and years of experience working with WUI participants, and reflecting on what I refer to as "Thotte's" (Otte's thoughts), I continually return to my lifelong experiences with gardening. It is clear to me that to grow great organizations, we must focus on the people—the plants, if you will. This includes everything from selecting the right environment and the right plants to fertilizing, pruning, weeding, and sometimes transplanting.

In his 2003 *Barron's* article "Breaking the Glass," columnist Gene Epstein wrote: "Women last year accounted for one out of 13 clout positions. . . . *Barron's* estimates that one in seven powerful posts will be held by women by 2010, based on evidence that the trend is getting only stronger. By 2020, it could be one in five." Though there is still a long way to go, I have noticed, through my corporate and WUI experiences, enormous positive changes in women's roles in the workplace. As more and more women enter the workplace, there will be more opportunities for more of them to become leaders. How they lead will have a major impact on the corporate landscape.

Changing the Corporate Landscape is divided into four sections:

- **SECTION I** focuses on trends and opportunities for women in the workplace and the role of leaders in developing leadership excellence.
- **SECTION II** focuses on the leader's need to create an inclusive and diverse workplace environment with ongoing support systems conducive to individual and organizational growth and success.
- **SECTION III** focuses on the leader's need to develop and sustain individual and organizational growth.
- **SECTION IV** focuses on the leader's need to continuously assess, improve, and sustain individual performance and organizational achievement.

In the chapters to follow, you will read about what it takes to cultivate leadership excellence and you will be able to reflect on your strengths and opportunities for improvement as a leader and role model for those around you.

SECTION I
THE LEADER

CHAPTER ONE

THE GARDENER AS LEADER

CHAPTER 1

THE GARDENER AS LEADER

"All too often we're giving people cut flowers, when we should be teaching them to grow their own plants."

—John Gardner

Whether tending a garden or an organization, it takes a knowledgeable, dedicated gardener or leader to help plants or people bloom and grow. An example of the parallel between the two is best illustrated by my dear friend from England, Valeria Pinder. Val, a former executive with Perot Systems Inc., and currently a London magistrate, has one of those beautiful picture-perfect English gardens. I refer to Val as the "garden nanny." She is a member of England's Royal Horticultural Society, and has a genuine love for what she does and an expertise in caring for her garden.

No matter what the time of year, Val is always hard at work in her garden, whether it is tending hundreds of seedlings in her greenhouse or pruning, transplanting, and weeding to ensure that her plants continue to thrive. As Val says,

"Gardening isn't something you do once a year and then sit back to admire. The garden needs a gardener who is willing to devote the time and energy, and who knows what needs to be done and when, throughout the year. The garden doesn't just take care of itself." Val has evolved and grown into a more competent gardener over the years, learning from her own successes and mistakes, as well as from those of other gardeners. As her expertise has evolved, so has her garden. In other words, the better the gardener, the better the garden. The same holds true in the workplace. How a leader leads affects an organization's success.

I designed the WOMEN Unlimited Inc. (WUI) programs to help organizations and their achievement-oriented women develop and strengthen their leadership skills. So much of what is learned in those programs is a result of shared workplace issues and achievements. One of the liveliest work-related discussions at WUI programs is about the best and worst jobs the participants have experienced. Interestingly, in both situations, so much had to do with how participants were treated as employees. In the garden, maltreated plants do not flourish any more than maltreated employees in an office do.

LEADERSHIP VERSUS MANAGEMENT

In his *Harvard Business Review* article "What Leaders Really Do," John P. Cotter asks readers to consider the following military analogy: ". . . a peacetime army can usually survive with good administration and management up and down the hierarchy, coupled with good leadership concentrated at the very top. A wartime army, however, needs competent leadership at all levels. No one yet has figured out how to manage people effectively into battle; they must be led."

It is astounding how the fundamentals of human nature get lost in business today. Employees want employers to make a connection with them, to care about what they think and care about what motivates them. When that occurs, the drive to excel is palpable. The business results reach extraordinary heights. When a leader has a visceral belief in the people in the organization, and makes decisions accordingly, a successful outcome is assured.

One of my very first experiences with leadership in the corporate world took place when I was an eager young woman being offered an entry-level management position in a customer service department of a world-renowned corporation. As the personnel manager ended the interview, he told me the job was a good one and he knew I would do well, but that I would be working for a very tough boss. I, of course, did not believe this would be a problem. I would do a wonderful job and the boss would be pleased with me. That was that. Had I met the boss ahead of time, I would have known differently. In those days, it was not common practice for potential employees to meet with the people to whom they would report.

As it turned out, "tough boss" was an inadequate description. After 18 months of indescribable abuse, I fled a job I could have enjoyed, feeling powerless and shaken. This experience was one of the first opportunities for me to learn and grow from an adverse situation in the workplace. I began a new job search and interviewed for another customer service position at the headquarters of McDonald's in Oakbrook, Illinois. During the second interview, I met the head of the department within which I would work, and was introduced to potential coworkers. Ray Kroc, McDonald's founder, and his management team had created a workplace environment in which employees were given opportunities to grow and contribute. I knew I wanted to work for that organization. After accepting the job, I flourished there.

Given equal ability in managing processes and achieving results, the most effective leader, whether male or female, is the person who values and is committed to relationship management. Leaders are not afraid to roll up their sleeves and do the hard work, and are acknowledged as wonderful people-developers. Effective leaders also have the ability to assess various situations and use the most effective style of leadership for the occasion—what is often referred to as situational leadership. Michele Coleman Mayes, now senior vice president and general counsel for Pitney Bowes, was previously head of the litigation department for Unisys, which was the result of a merger between Burroughs Corporation and Sperry Corporation. She was responsible for creating a team made up of Sperry attorneys, relocated attorneys from Burroughs, and new attorneys hired for the new company. Zenola Harper, vice president and senior counsel, litigation, for Bristol-Myers Squibb Company, worked with Michele at the time and recalls one staff meeting in particular that stands out as an example of Michele's role as a situational leader. "One of my colleagues was particularly challenging and bordered on disrespectful in the meeting," said Zenola. "Michele knew that she could escalate the situation like oil on fire, or she could tackle the issue without embarrassing my colleague in public. Certainly, most of the staff thought it appropriate to put our colleague in his place. However, Michele diffused the situation and later dealt with our colleague in private, one-on-one. Her ability to defer and diffuse that battle left a strong impression on me as being an important trait of a good leader."

"UNLIKE MANAGERS, LEADERS FOCUS ON THE PEOPLE WHO HAVE TO ACHIEVE THE PROCESS."

Unlike managers, leaders focus on the people who have to achieve the process. The "tough manager" I mentioned earlier is an example of someone who abused the people involved in the process. He certainly was not a leader. Leaders such as Michele recognize the difference between managing and leading. Although leaders and managers manage a process, only leaders lead.

A Changing Landscape

During my years in the corporate world, and as founder of WUI, I have had the opportunity to observe what contributes to the success of outstanding leaders. Until recent years, most business leaders have been men. As more women enter the corporate world, the corporate landscape changes.

According to the "Women in U.S. Corporate Leadership: 2003" study done by Catalyst, a research and advisory organization committed to advancing women in business, "While women accounted for only 8.7 percent of corporate officers in 1995, they represented 15.7 percent in 2002. Women's low 1.2-percent representation amongst Fortune 500 top earners grew to 5.2 percent by 2002. And at the very top, the Fortune 500 claimed one woman CEO in 1995, and [in 2002] there [were] seven—an increase from 0.2 percent to 1.4 percent."

It is particularly interesting to observe the recent focus on women and their leadership abilities. One has only to look at the ongoing scrutiny of the highly acclaimed Carly Fiorina, CEO of Hewlett-Packard, or Martha Stewart, and the multimedia coverage of their leadership abilities and flaws, to see how much interest there is in how women lead. In addition, coverage of Anne Mulcahy of Xerox, Ann Fudge of Young & Rubicam, Betsy Holden of Kraft Foods, Andrea Yung of Avon, and Lois Juliber of Colgate-Palmolive all discussed what women might bring to the table versus their male counterparts. Are women more collaborative? Are men more competitive? Are women better communicators? These articles state that women might be more flexible in the way the work environment operates, and that the workplace could become more productive with women leaders.

So, does all this mean that women are better leaders than men? Will there be a major shift in how businesses are run?

Effective leadership is not a gender issue. Throughout my years in the business world, I have seen both outstanding and ineffective leaders, whether male or female. All successful leaders have one major "thread of similarity." They are highly motivated and skilled in aspects of basic leadership—a clear vision focused on results, a broad perspective and knowledge of the business—and they clearly understand and value the needs of their internal and external customers. Their internal customers are their employees. Leaders foster an environment in which the needs of both types of customers are met. They constantly listen to the voice of their customers. They are flexible and adaptable in making the changes that are in the best interest of both the organization and their customers.

"SUCCESS IS AN EQUAL OPPORTUNITY EMPLOYER—BOTH MEN AND WOMEN HAVE THE OPPORTUNITY TO BE SUCCESSFUL."

Corporate America is certainly not as male dominated as when I first entered it. Success is an equal opportunity employer—both men and women have the opportunity to be successful. Conversely, both can experience career derailment. Oftentimes, their leadership styles result in their inability to gain the support they need to achieve results.

THE OLD GUARD

In her book, *Why the Best Man for the Job Is a Woman,* Esther Wachs Book reviews two highly criticized executive women: Jill Barad, former chief executive of Mattel, and Linda Wachner, of Warnaco. These two women were identified as the "paradigm of old leadership." Both "paved the way for the success of other women by rising through the ranks of some of America's leading corporations." However, "the manner in which Barad used to run Mattel and that which Wachner employs at Warnaco . . . put them at a disadvantage in today's changing world. Their management styles hampered their progress and their ability to grasp the need for change."

I would add to Book's analysis of these two highly skilled women that, as with many other early female business pioneers, their role model for leadership was that of the old male model: "I am the boss, do as I say!" Remember those old movies in which most women executives were portrayed as tough, unlikable women, who sacrificed everything to achieve the ultimate in their careers—the old Joan Crawford "Queen Bee" types?

Remember poor Melanie Griffith at the hands of tyrannical Sigourney Weaver in the movie *Working Girl*? Fortunately, this management style is becoming outdated. Many companies today are working toward creating a corporate landscape in which both male and female leaders are rewarded for attracting, retaining, and developing their employees, in addition to achieving bottom-line results. There is, however, still room for improvement. As in a garden, there is always work to be done to assure a bountiful harvest from one season to another.

Passing the Ball

How do children in a new neighborhood meet other children? Having moved to a number of new neighborhoods as a child, I remember what it was like to look outside and see the other children playing games, and wanting to join. The question was always: How do I get invited into the game? How do I get the other kids to pass me the ball?

Like adults, children often look at what others contribute to the group. Is the new person someone they would like to have join them? Will the individual get along and help achieve the results they are looking for? Does the individual look prepared to play the game? It is the same in business. The "players" want to know what you have to offer. In business, however, it is often tougher to be invited to join the game. Not only are you competing with others who wish to join the game, but there are more players you have to convince to pass you the ball.

Think about well-known athletes. Some are the MVP one year and traded the following year. Along comes a new player, who scores more baskets or makes more touchdowns, and the former MVP is in the position of proving his or her abilities to the other players and fans all over again.

Ilene Lang, president of Catalyst, was one of a handful of senior women at a prominent tech company in the early 1990s. All of the women were aware that their industry lacked networking opportunities for women. "As successful women, we knew we had the power to change this," said Lang. "We organized a network of women directors and senior staff to mentor women and show them new growth opportunities. And, we didn't stop there. We made a pact: We would personally keep tabs on all the women directors and managers at the company and not let a single high-performing woman leave the company without one of us trying to help her stay." When a woman announced she was leaving, Lang and her colleagues would ask the woman why she was leaving. What did she want to do with her career? How could they help her stay? They were successful in bringing back a star employee, in getting two women promoted from director to vice president, and in "saving" a few top performers who were ready to walk out the door. "By making that pact," said Lang, "we not only managed to help women advance, but we also stocked our own personal networks with successful women."

One way leaders ensure success in their own career is by contributing to the success of others. In her book *She Wins, You Win,* Gail Evans said: "Every time a woman succeeds in business, every other woman's chance of succeeding in business increases. Every time a woman fails in business, every other woman's chance of failure increases." By passing others the ball, helping them develop their ball-handling skills, and offering opportunities for others to "score," leaders ensure the success of the group. In gardening, legumes take nitrogen from the air to nurture themselves. When planted next to root vegetables, the nitrogen the legumes add to the soil also benefits the plants around them. As John Nash's character in the movie *A Beautiful Mind*, says, "The best result comes from everyone in the group doing what is best for himself and the group."

> "EVERY TIME A WOMAN SUCCEEDS IN BUSINESS, EVERY OTHER WOMAN'S CHANCE OF SUCCEEDING IN BUSINESS INCREASES. EVERY TIME A WOMAN FAILS IN BUSINESS, EVERY OTHER WOMAN'S CHANCE OF FAILURE INCREASES."

TALENT RETENTION

In recent years, I have seen many highly talented women leave or think about leaving corporate America. In the summer 2003 edition of *Executive Female* magazine, the article "Why Women Leave" states: "Corporate culture is the number one reason why women flee executive posts. . . . Respondents expressed disappointment in closed management styles that marginalized, micromanaged and/or denigrated their work and felt excluded from informal networks." There can be no doubt that with the number of women who are electing to start their own businesses, there needs to be a greater emphasis on retaining achievement-oriented women in corporate America. According to the Center for Women's Business Research, in May 2003, nearly half of all privately held United States businesses were women-owned.

In his *Harvard Business Review* article "Winning the Talent War for Women," Douglas M. McCracken, former chairman of Deloitte & Touche LLP, United States, and former chief executive officer of Deloitte Consulting, discussed how women were "leaving the firm at a significantly greater rate than men" in the 1990s.

Deloitte & Touche analyzed the situation and changed its approach to retaining talented women. It took a "cultural revolution," said McCracken. And as a result, the "firm's annual turnover rate as a whole fell from around 25 percent in the early 1990s to 18 percent in 1999, despite an intensifying war for talent," he said. Lower turnover also saved Deloitte & Touche $250 million in hiring and training costs.

I have had many discussions on this issue with women who tell me they do not believe their contribution to their organization is valued. Many believe their voice is not heard in the decision-making process. For years it has been my personal belief that companies are missing the boat when they do not have women help design products and services, particularly since so many products and services are bought by women. According to

WOW (Wider Opportunities for Women) Facts 2002, "Women influence the purchase of 80% of all consumer goods." In his most recent book, *Re-imagine! Business Excellence in a Disruptive Age,* leadership guru Tom Peters asks readers to "Wake up about the power of women: as managers, leaders and consumers. Companies are essentially turning away business by not tapping this potential."

It is clear that an organization's leadership team—particularly those who design the products and services and represent the organization to the consumers—must represent the diversity of its consumer base. Organizations and today's leaders must continue to develop women and other minorities in the corporate landscape—not only because it is the right thing to do, but because it is in the best interest of the organizations to do so. History has shown that any significant organizational initiative or change requires the commitment of an outstanding leader.

The Faces of Leadership

What is the difference between good and great leadership? Why is one leader considered capable and another outstanding? When WUI participants are asked to name the leaders they most admire, they usually respond with names such as Winston Churchill, Mahatma Gandhi, John F. Kennedy, Martin Luther King, Jr., Jesus, Eleanor Roosevelt, and Oprah Winfrey. It is interesting to note how different these leaders are from each other. Gandhi and Churchill, two highly recognized world leaders, possessed different styles and came from different backgrounds, yet both were able to rally the support of the people in their respective countries and around the world. What is the common denominator? They both inspired others.

> "WHAT IS THE DIFFERENCE BETWEEN GOOD AND GREAT LEADERSHIP?"

As mentioned earlier, the most admired leaders are usually outstanding people developers who others want to follow. They understand the importance of making people feel valued. In his *Harvard Business Review* article "What Makes a Leader?" Daniel Goleman, the celebrated author of *Emotional Intelligence,* wrote: "[T]he most effective leaders are alike in one crucial way: they all have a high degree of what has come to be known as *emotional intelligence.* It is not that IQ and technical skills are irrelevant. They do matter, but mainly as 'threshold capabilities'; that is, they are the entry-level requirements for executive positions. . . . [E]motional intelligence is the sine qua non of leadership. Without it, a person can have the best training in the world, an incisive, analytical mind, and an endless supply of smart ideas, but he still won't make a great leader." Goleman identifies the components of emotional intelligence as self-awareness, self-regulation, motivation, empathy, and social skill.

The WUI programs focus on the "emotional intelligence" aspect of leadership and encourage the participants to hone those skills in addition to the basic business skills required. It has been my privilege to have met many wonderful men and women who exemplify leadership excellence. Although *Changing the Corporate Landscape* features a wide variety of leaders, there are seven in particular who I've chosen to focus on more extensively: Karen Nemetz Duvall, Sandy Beach Lin, Michele Coleman Mayes, Debbie Murphy, Susan Sobbott, Betsy Wanner, and John L. "Jack" Yurish. They represent diverse personal and professional backgrounds, genders, ages, and races, yet all share that "thread of similarity" that makes them quintessential leaders. Karen is a partner, business operations, of Clarus Health LLC and former executive vice president of Toys R Us. Sandy is the president of Alcoa Closure Systems International and a member of the Committee of 200. Michele, who was introduced above in the "Leadership versus Management" section, is a 2003 recipient of the prestigious Margaret Brent Women Lawyers of Achievement Award in addition to being senior vice president and general counsel at Pitney Bowes. Debbie Murphy is former vice president of global strategic alliances for IBM Sales & Distribution Group. Susan Sobbott is a senior vice president and general manager at the American Express Company. Betsy Wanner is a vice president at the Walt Disney Company. Jack Yurish is the

> "LEADERSHIP IS ABOUT MORE THAN JUST DELIVERING RESULTS—IT IS ABOUT MAKING A DIFFERENCE IN THE LIVES OF OTHERS."

founder and chairman of the Cambridge Management Institute and former senior executive and owner of National Car Rental Systems Inc.

There is more to each of these leaders than their titles. They all share the belief that leadership is about more than just delivering results—it is about making a difference in the lives of others. Throughout *Changing the Corporate Landscape*, examples of their wisdom and expertise, highlighting why they are successful leaders and people developers, will be shared. Based on their example of leadership, and the emerging trends in leadership, it is clear that leadership excellence requires:

- VISION
- PRESENCE
- INTEGRITY
- FOSTERING A SUPPORTIVE ENVIRONMENT
- BEING ORGANIZATIONALLY SAVVY
- CREATING AND MAINTAINING STRATEGIC ALLIANCES
- INFLUENCING AND NEGOTIATING
- ADVERSITY MANAGEMENT
- MAKING TOUGH DECISIONS
- FLEXIBILITY, ADAPTABILITY, AND APPROACHABILITY
- REFLECTION, REASSESSMENT, AND RENEWAL
- ROLE MODELS

VISION

Leaders are able to clearly define a desired future outcome. They possess the ability to communicate that vision to motivate and inspire others at all levels of the organization. As a leader, it is essential to create a shared vision. Today, Oprah Winfrey is one of the most well-known mainstream visionary leaders. Through her television program and her magazine, she has shared her vision of a better life and inspired others to work toward achieving that vision with her—be it through self-improvement or improving the lives of others. Sandy Beach Lin had an opportunity to meet her at a large conference at which she was speaking. "I was amazed at how she took time to look into each person's eyes and listen to what each person had to say," said Sandy. "To me, this embodied what a strong leader does—gets her message across, listens to the people around her and executes her vision."

PRESENCE

Leaders must project an image of competence and confidence. There is no doubt that we never get a second chance to make a first impression. We have all seen people who walk into a room and immediately command the attention of the room and are admired. They have "it." How people perceive us is their reality of us, and as leaders it is vital that we project an image of competence and confidence. In Michelle Conlin's July 22, 2002 *Business Week* article, "She's Gotta Have 'It,'" she states:

"'It,' in this case, is executive presence, the elusive quality that has over the past year become a major focus in women's leadership development circles. This trait is so important to companies such as Shell Group and J.P. Morgan Chase that they have packed off their high-potential female managers to special seminars to develop 'it'. . . ." The article goes on to say that executive presence is a "key to unlocking women's advancement."

> "LEADERS ARE ABLE TO CLEARLY DEFINE A DESIRED FUTURE OUTCOME."

The famous Kennedy/Nixon televised debates of the sixties exemplify the power of presence. Kennedy clearly portrayed an aura of confidence and competence, whereas Nixon displayed the opposite. He looked so uncomfortable, and the way in which he projected himself left many uninspired and questioning his abilities. More recently, Arnold Schwarzenegger's gubernatorial campaign and Howard Dean's presidential campaign provide examples of the importance of presence and how it can be an asset or a derailer.

INTEGRITY

Leaders are honest, ethical, fair, courageous, and accountable. Not one of us would want to say that we are people who operate without integrity. But we have to ask ourselves these questions: Do we always truly act with complete integrity in the business arena? Do we always stand up for what we believe is the right thing to do? Are we always operating in a fair and ethical manner? Are we accountable? Do we take responsibility for our actions or for the actions of our employees? Do we walk the talk? Do our actions match our words?

When Beth Ziff, president of Customer Care Inc., worked with Jim Barksdale in the mid-1990s, he was the CEO of AT&T. At the time, Beth was responsible for the organization's customer service group. Jim made her feel that her focus was the most important and far-reaching in the company; and he impressed upon her why it was so important to embody integrity and live the "golden rule" when he shared a story about applying for an Exxon credit card when he was in college.

> "DO OUR ACTIONS MATCH OUR WORDS?"

"He was rejected for the card and actually called the company to ask why," said Beth. "When explaining why he was denied, the customer service person was rude to him. Jim never forgot the experience. Several years later, when he was the CEO of FedEx, several companies were vying for the fuel contracts for FedEx airplanes. When he rejected Exxon, they asked why, and he recounted his college experience."

FOSTERING A SUPPORTIVE ENVIRONMENT

Leaders create an environment that values diversity and fosters, acknowledges, and rewards growth. They manage at macro rather than micro levels, actively pursue diversity, and are acknowledged people-developers; they recognize and reward people for their contributions, empower and support others, and are the individuals whom people in the rest of their organizations want to work for.

To be successful in this area, Debbie Murphy said, "a leader must create an environment in which the employees feel comfortable bringing problems forward." As Carl W. Buechner said, "They may forget what you said, but they will never forget how you made them feel."

BEING ORGANIZATIONALLY SAVVY

Leaders know the unwritten "rules of the game." Basic business skills and competence are required to gain entry into the "game." This does not mean, however, that you will automatically get to play or win! Leaders understand the organization's structure and how it operates. They are able to successfully navigate up, down, and across the organization and know how to achieve results with and through others. "Organizational savvy is critical to success in today's business environment," said Denise Yohn, vice president of segment marketing and brand planning for Sony Electronics Incorporated. Organizationally savvy people identify very quickly what the corporate culture is, what the values, the goals, the attitudes of the company are, and then work toward demonstrating what they support and how they can contribute.

"LEADERS KNOW THE UNWRITTEN 'RULES OF THE GAME.'"

CREATING AND MAINTAINING STRATEGIC ALLIANCES

Leaders have networks established at all levels of the organization; they know who keeps score, who the players are, and who can help them. They understand the importance of helping others with their agendas and know how much they can learn from others. When asked what contributed to her success as a leader, Sandy Beach Lin answered that tenacity was first, but that the ability to build and grow teams (forms of strategic alliances) was second. "I know as a leader that I must surround myself with talented people and rely on others, so the ability to choose good talent and develop leaders has served me well," said Sandy.

INFLUENCING AND NEGOTIATING

Leaders are able to motivate, influence, and negotiate at all levels to achieve a mutually beneficial outcome. They respect and value the opinions of others. When Bob Danzig, who retired after twenty years as the head of the Hearst Newspaper Group and vice president of the Hearst Corporation, became the publisher of the Albany *Times Union*, the newspaper was "plagued with executive competition." At weekly management sessions, Bob noticed how the executives guarded their own departmental turf and bristled when other managers made suggestions for departments outside their own. "The net effect," said Bob, "was a type of paralysis that allowed the company to function each day, but inhibited any collective quest for new growth. Not one of the executives was a force for progress in the collective purpose of the newspaper since all their concentration was on their own feet—in their own shoes exclusively."

After a few weeks of struggling with the tensions, Bob approached the American Press Institute, a newspaper executive development resource. He asked that executives be permitted to attend sessions in areas of responsibility different from their own. For example, an editor would attend a session for advertising managers. When Bob told the competing managers that they would be attending these sessions and learn to "walk in the other person's shoes," reaction was universally negative. "Within a few months of genuinely learning about the challenges of each other's specialty areas," said Bob, "they began a new language of insight, understanding, and cooperation. Within six months, we had committees working collectively on new horizons." Bob's ability to influence and negotiate within different departments at the newspaper led to a new culture and spirit of cooperation at the *Times Union*.

ADVERSITY MANAGEMENT

Leaders maintain stability in adverse situations by planning and managing adverse consequences up front. They project competence and confidence to those around them. They focus on solving the problem, not assigning blame. In addition to having knowledge of the business or of processes that may potentially have some type of problem, a good leader does the upfront work, examining all the potential barriers and problems that could occur, and making plans for what might have to happen in the event of any type of breakdown in the process.

> "LEADERS MAINTAIN STABILITY IN ADVERSE SITUATIONS BY PLANNING AND MANAGING ADVERSE CONSEQUENCES UP FRONT."

I have always advocated for this particular skill being considered one that separates the successful leader from the unsuccessful leader. In fact, I would go so far as to say that leaders who really do well in this area get additional points, if you will, for their skill level. After all, leaders who inspire others and help them during times of crisis are the ones who are always the most looked up to. They deal with the issues in a very calm, very cool, and very confident manner.

When Pamela Robinson, director, global solution sales discipline leader, IBM, describes Debbie Murphy, she describes her as "calm, cool, and collected, like a duck gliding effortlessly across a pond." The "duck" is something Debbie shares as a piece of advice to women. "In my first management position within IBM, one of my early mentors gave me this advice, which I have followed throughout my management and executive career," said Debbie. "A duck on the water crosses the water very smoothly, with its head held high, poised and confident, while underneath, its feet are paddling like crazy to propel itself. A successful leader is one who is calm, confident, and poised no matter what may be churning inside. This behavior permeates the organization very successfully."

MAKING TOUGH DECISIONS

Jill Kanin-Lovers, senior vice president of human resources for Avon Products Inc., works with Andrea Jung, CEO of Avon. "Similar to many of us, [Andrea] likes to be liked. However, this is tough in an organization that needs to go through significant change," said Jill. "Andrea Jung has mastered the people aspect of tough decision-making by, first, being quite up front about her derailer, but at the same time committing to the organization that she will do what it takes to make the right leadership calls. Second, she has made each leadership decision with full transparency." In other words, expectations have been clearly articulated.

Part of making tough decisions is also asking for input from others. "It's comforting to know that when you ask a senior executive about his or her toughest decision, they almost always involve people," said Karen Nemetz Duvall. "How these decisions are handled separates the administrators from the leaders."

FLEXIBILITY, ADAPTABILITY, AND APPROACHABILITY

Leaders are not resistant to change, and they adapt easily when the situation requires change. They are not feared. They are respected individuals who can interact comfortably with a diverse customer base and workforce. Being flexible and adaptable certainly does not mean lacking conviction. The most successful leaders clearly stay the course, keep their focus, and march toward an outcome that will be beneficial for all. However, the best leaders I have ever had the pleasure of working with were always the ones that were able not only to make change when necessary but to recognize that change can often result in opportunities for something better as a result. In fact, Sandy Beach Lin attributes her success to, among other things, her flexibility; while Michele Coleman Mayes said that her willingness to try new things was one of the greatest contributors to her success.

One of the best examples I have of watching flexible and adaptable leaders achieve success took place during one of the first acquisitions of NCR. There were many department heads who had been with the company for a very long time and were very happy with their situation and with how the company was being run. When management faced turning the company in a very different direction—it was in fact going to be innovative in the industry; it was going to become far more of a marketing-type organization than it had been—it was the flexible and adaptable employees who made the transition. Many of the department heads at that time resisted—and resisted to the extent that they became almost nonproductive. They certainly did not inspire confidence in their employees, nor was it a motivator for their

> "LEADERS ARE NOT RESISTANT TO CHANGE, AND THEY ADAPT EASILY WHEN THE SITUATION REQUIRES CHANGE."

employees to see their managers resisting everything they were being asked to do and digging in their heels with an attitude of "if it ain't broke, don't fix it." Sadly, many of those individuals were asked to leave the organization to make room for leaders who would embrace the new value system and the new direction.

Leaders must also be approachable. They must be respected because of the way they interact with people, engendering admiration, not fear. I am reminded of the "emperor with no clothes" syndrome. There are still leaders in corporate America that people will tell only good news to because they fear the reaction of the leader who does not want to hear anything but positive news. These are the leaders who inspire the yes-men and -women.

REFLECTION, REASSESSMENT, AND RENEWAL

Leaders consistently step back to reflect and gain perspective on what, why, and how well they are leading in order to maintain their leadership excellence and passion for what they do. This skill set is, sadly, one of the least used by and most needed for leaders, who must retain their sense of commitment, passion, contribution, and personal development if they are to continue being successful leaders.

It is essential, for many reasons, for them to take a step back and take a "30,000 feet" view of what they are doing. One reason, of course, is to avoid the stress and burnout that occurs when leaders become caught up in the vortex of the 24/7 business world. With the technology now available, many leaders have become addicted to e-mail and voice mail. For example, I often hear messages and read e-mails that were sent in the wee small hours of the morning. Working around the clock on a continuous basis will, of course, adversely affect the well-being of leaders who engage in this behavior. It will also ultimately have an adverse affect on workplace performance.

Overtired, stressed leaders make errors in judgment and, as I share with the women in our program, they certainly are not a joy to be around either at work or at home. I have this picture in my head of Miss Gulch on her bike in *The Wizard of Oz.* I can hear the frenetic music playing as she peddles like crazy. This is how I visualize many women in the workplace as they attempt to do what is often unrealistic and unnecessary!

Heather Lawley, strategic alliances field marketing manager for Cisco Systems Inc., believes that "many women, in their endeavor to be 'taken seriously,' go overboard on the competency piece. Yes, competency is always a core requirement. However, it is the personality that makes each of us unique and breathes life into the content. And frankly, it make us more approachable, likeable, and human."

ROLE MODELS

One of the most important aspects of leadership, of course, is that leaders must be role models for the next generation. They need to propagate both new leaders and new followers. Clearly, the leader who can score high marks in all of the attributes and skills that we just discussed will be, and is, in fact, the role model for the next generation of leaders.

SUMMARY

Leaders must pay equal attention to achieving business results and developing people. "As a leader," said Debbie Murphy, "I believe it is critical to build loyalty within the organization, which will then create a high-performing environment in which your employees can excel. This takes personal time and energy from the leader by being very visible to the employees, knowing each of them by their first name, including them in key decision-making or goal-setting, and reinforcing the achievement of goals on a regular basis. To be successful in this area, a leader must create an environment where the employees feel comfortable to bring problems forward because they know the leader will listen and work as a team to solve the problem. And, the leader needs to recognize the talents of the employees by giving them additional leadership assignments to grow their experience, and then letting the employees work independently to complete those assignments with guidance from the leader where needed. If leaders can earn the respect and loyalty of their employees by personally working at it every day, the whole organization can be successful and be a place where people want to work and thrive."

In summary, it is clear that leadership excellence requires:

- Vision
- Presence
- Integrity
- Fostering a supportive environment
- Being organizationally savvy
- Creating and maintaining strategic alliances
- Influencing and negotiating
- Adversity management
- Making tough decisions
- Flexibility, adaptability, and approachability
- Reflection, reassessment, and renewal
- Role models

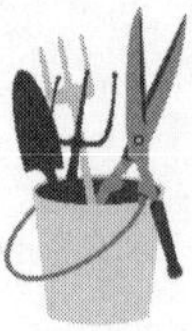

Leadership Inventory

1. Do you recognize and value the importance of your being knowledgeable regarding trends and opportunities for women in the workplace?

What have you identified as the important trends and opportunities for your leadership and career development?

What resources/activities help you to stay informed and enable you to act upon these trends and opportunities?

When was the last time you used these resources to further your knowledge of workplace trends and opportunities?

2. Do you recognize and value the importance and need for you to continuously develop your leadership skills?

What actions have you taken to develop those skills?

How has this contributed to your growth and development?

What resources/activities help you in the achievement of this goal?

When was the last time you used those resources or participated in an activity to further your leadership knowledge and skills?

3. Do you recognize and value the need for the leader to be a role model for the next generation of leaders?

What actions have you taken to fulfill this role?

How has this contributed to your growth and development?

What resources/activities help you in the achievement of this goal?

When was the last time you used those resources or participated in an activity to further the growth of others?

4. Review the leadership skills criteria identified in Chapter 1. Identify those criteria you consider your strengths.

Identify those criteria you consider your areas of opportunity for improvement.

CALL TO ACTION

Based upon your response to the Leadership Inventory, identify three (3) actions to further your continuing development and success as a leader.

Action	Timetable
1.	
2.	
3.	

CHAPTER TWO

HOW WILL YOUR GARDEN GROW?

CHAPTER 2

HOW WILL YOUR GARDEN GROW?

> *"The future belongs to those who believe in the beauty of their dreams."*
>
> *—Eleanor Roosevelt*

I am in awe of the visionaries who created such gardens as those at Versailles. They designed the many acres of trees and flowers, fountains and reflecting pools, without computers to design blueprints or the other time-saving equipment we have today, transforming their visions into acre upon acre of beautiful gardens. What they did have was the ability to define their visions and inspire others to embrace, help create, and maintain their visions—something all successful leaders do.

When asked about vision and the ability to create a shared vision with others in the corporate world, Karen Nemetz Duvall said: "It doesn't take long for a seasoned leader to envision what the organization looks like when the transformation is complete. Translating the vision into an emotionally and intellectually inspiring message to a broad audience is a true gift. One of my most admired mentors described the transformation in our company as 'moving to the house on the hill.' Most corporate lifers can relate to the anxiety of moving our families to a new home. Think about the relief when we have found the new home, have tackled the overwhelming plan to get there and know exactly where our valued treasures will be placed. Enormous energy is released and all efforts are on packing up and moving on. Some may be satisfied with identifying the neighborhood, but many need to know exactly where that blue couch is going. The most visionary communicators get to the blue couch very quickly."

> "THE MOST VISIONARY COMMUNICATORS GET TO THE BLUE COUCH VERY QUICKLY."

GETTING TO THE BLUE COUCH

Leaders designing a new corporate landscape need to have a very clear vision of what that landscape will look like and what they as leaders need to do to create it, in the same way that a gardener needs to look at a landscape and decide what needs to be planted to create the desired garden.

Throughout history, there have been many men and women who have had a clear vision of what they wanted to accomplish. One has only to think of history's early explorers, inventors, and scholars, such as Christopher Columbus, Amelia Earhart, Marie

Curie, and Alexander Graham Bell, to name a few. When I fly from the United States' East Coast to the West Coast, I often think about those early pioneers who crossed this vast land in pursuit of their vision of a new and better life. When one considers the dreadful adversity they encountered, it is to their credit that they kept going. Their vision for a better life was what drove so many of them to finish their journey. The same can be said about the millions who left their homes during the early 1900s to seek better lives in new countries.

When I think of more recent visionaries, I think about Martin Luther King, Jr. It is hard to forget his "I Have a Dream" speech and what that call to action did for the civil rights movement. In the business world, individuals such as Walt Disney come to mind for their persistence and dedication to achieving their visions. Disney's vision resulted in bringing pleasure to so many and creating an industry employing thousands around the world. As Disney said, "If you can dream it, you can do it. Always remember this whole thing started with a mouse." Oprah Winfrey is another example of someone who has inspired and brought hope to millions around the world.

Simply having a vision does not ensure that a person's vision will be achieved. As Steve Case, former chairman and chief executive officer of America Online Inc. and AOL Time Warner, said, "Vision in the absence of execution is hallucination." With a garden, someone must develop the vision, determine how it will be achieved, and then plant it and care for it continuously with actions. The difference between those who achieve their vision and those who fail is most often due to the achieving individual's ability to create a shared vision. They must have desire, commitment, persistence, and flexibility, and the ability to identify the necessary actions and establish a process to achieve the vision. How many times have you seen a new product or service advertised and said to yourself, "I was going to do that. I had that idea years ago." If you do not act upon your idea, someone else will.

> "VISION IN THE ABSENCE OF EXECUTION IS HALLUCINATION."

When I've asked others why they haven't done anything with the dreams they've shared with me, the answers are varied, but the most common is: "I didn't know how and now it is too late." In the words of George Eliot: "It's never too late to be what you might have been."

FOSTERING A SHARED VISION

In their book *Because of You,* authors Dan Zadra and Katie Lambert say, "Northern geese travel thousands of miles in perfect formation. . . . As each of the great birds moves its wings, it creates a steady uplift for the bird behind it. Formation flying is 70 percent more efficient than flying alone." In small gardens, gardeners are often able to manage their garden independently. But large gardens such as Wisley, the Royal Horticultural

Society's garden in Surrey, England; Giverny, Claude Monet's farmhouse garden in Eure, France; or Dumbarton Oaks, located in Washington, D.C., are a reflection of shared vision and action. Although these gardens may be based on the vision of a few individuals, it takes numerous individuals to implement and maintain the visions.

> "FORMATION FLYING IS 70 PERCENT MORE EFFICIENT THAN FLYING ALONE."

Leaders in the corporate world are often required to have a vision of new products and services. In these days of reengineering and downsizing in so many corporations, the leader must continuously envision how to do more with less. They have to obtain "buy-in" from others—they need employees who have a vested interest in their visions. Professionals who share a common direction and sense of community draw upon each other's strengths. Formation flying is a demonstration of shared vision that enables both the leaders and their followers to reach their final destination in a more efficient manner.

I stress the importance of sharing a vision in terms others can relate to because it was during WUI's building process that I came to realize how willing most people are to be helpful when they understand and support a vision—especially if it is clearly communicated and viewed as a benefit. As Mary Kay Ash, the founder of the very successful Mary Kay Cosmetics, said: "A mediocre idea that generates enthusiasm will go further than a great idea that inspires no one."

I had numerous conversations in those early days of WUI with the people who supported me. It was extremely important that they be given the opportunity to question, give their recommendations, and state their concerns. Simply telling people about one's vision is not the way to obtain buy-in. In attempting to gain buy-in and ongoing support, it is essential to listen, suspend judgment if and when people push back or question, and be open to the probability that they will add even more possibilities to your picture. When people are given that opportunity, and feel they are integral to the success of achieving the vision, they are most likely to contribute beyond what you may expect.

> "A MEDIOCRE IDEA THAT GENERATES ENTHUSIASM WILL GO FURTHER THAN A GREAT IDEA THAT INSPIRES NO ONE."

In establishing a shared vision, you have to have a clear view of your dreams, then develop a plan for action, establish support systems, and display flexibility, a positive attitude, and persistence. After leaving her position as a vice president for Toys R Us, Karen Nemetz Duvall established the company Clarus Health. At her previous position, Karen had been busy building the collective confidence of a new team during a critical turnaround. "We had completed the hard work of determining who and what we wanted to be and were committed to getting there. The real job for any visionary leader was just beginning and I began to wonder what it would be like to head an organization where the core values of the company were consistently and explicitly reflected in its culture, leadership principles and behaviors," she said. At the same time, Karen's future Clarus Health business partner was working for another large organization, envisioning a new business model.

They developed a plan for action and launched the business quietly and slowly. This gave them the flexibility to articulate their core values and differentiators and translate them into a meaningful vision while they got on the right track.

As they began to grow, they focused on their infrastructure. They built their benefits plan, people policies, and workspace to reinforce their values. Their systems, financial planning processes, and recruiting strategies were crafted around their vision. Every time they were faced with an ambiguous or complex decision, they went back to their initial vision for answers.

Two different corporate careers and visions led to the founding of Clarus Health. *Clarus* is a Latin word that means "to illuminate, clarify; to make bright." Karen and her partner are recognized in the industry for doing this well, because they apply the same effort to their own vision and values first.

IMAGINATION AND DREAMS

Can you imagine what it would have been like to be one of the first astronauts in space? They truly went where "no man has gone before." Although the astronauts had large support teams embracing the vision and taking the actions needed to send them into space, the astronauts had to invest in the vision of space and not allow their fears of the unknown to distract them.

When I first began to imagine what kind of career and business I would most like to create, I brainstormed every possible situation. It is important in the imagination stage to really let your ideas unfold without constructing "I could not do that" and "That would not work" roadblocks in your head. As Henry Ford said: "Obstacles are those frightful things you see when you take your eyes off your goal." Let your ideas flow. Only then will you know what most appeals to you or is most likely a vision you have a true desire to achieve.

> "OBSTACLES ARE THOSE FRIGHTFUL THINGS YOU SEE WHEN YOU TAKE YOUR EYES OFF YOUR GOAL."

It is also important at this stage to ask yourself two very important questions: What is the price that has to be paid to achieve this vision; and Am I willing to pay it? Establishing a vision as a reality takes a great deal of time and energy. In addition to the demands on yourself, how will this affect your family, friends, and colleagues? Are you able to give them the necessary time, energy, and commitment?

CLEAR COMMUNICATION

Clarifying your vision is the next step. It is important to define the specific results you want to achieve. In 1990, I began documenting how I envisioned the graduation of a WUI program and what the participants, mentors, and managers would say was the result of the experience. I envisioned what the workshops would offer, who would attend, and where they would be located. Long before that first program launched in New York City in April 1994, I had written pages and pages of ideas for how I would market the program, how I would describe what the program would offer, and how both the participants and the organization would benefit from the experience.

I remember the day I envisioned the WUI program as a learning experience similar to the Weight Watchers program. Participants would come to the first program and "weigh in." They would share their feedback from their leadership assessments and set goals for what they wanted to achieve. Over the year-long program, they would then be given the opportunity and support to achieve their goals and desired results, and they would be responsible for their own progress. They had to "weigh in" each month and would be held accountable by their team and mentors.

I based the program content on the feedback received from the men and women I interviewed over several years, as well as from the experiences I had as the leader of an organizational development department. In other words, I established at the outset what the outcome and measurement of success would be, before moving to the next step.

ACTION

Jean Monnet once said, "All people of great achievement are ambitious, but the key question [of character] is whether they are ambitious to *be* or ambitious to *do*." When it came to WUI, I was ambitious to *do*. With the help of Jack Yurish, my friend, mentor, and former boss at NCR, I developed short- and long-range action plans with three important questions assigned to every action/goal documented:

> "ALL PEOPLE OF GREAT ACHIEVEMENT ARE AMBITIOUS, BUT THE KEY QUESTION [OF CHARACTER] IS WHETHER THEY ARE AMBITIOUS TO **BE** OR AMBITIOUS TO **DO**."

- What/who could help me achieve this goal?
- What/who could prevent me from achieving this goal?
- How could I gain that support and how could I overcome those barriers?

Each action was assigned a timeline for completion and those plans became the document that dictated how I spent my time and, of course, became a measurement of my successes and failures. For example, I set ambitious timelines for actions, which often had to be redefined. For the most part, this was because I had been far too positive in my thinking that others would stick to my timelines. I can remember once setting up three appointments in one morning to share my vision of WUI, only to have the first appointment keep me waiting over an hour before seeing me. This resulted in my spending only five minutes with the first client and asking for a second meeting, and then rescheduling the third meeting of the day. When setting timelines, I learned that I have to consider what is realistic for others involved, and not just my own schedule.

One of the most crucial elements of this planning process was to engage others in the process. Not only to get a different perspective and their great ideas, but also to have them serve as a reality check and sounding board. On numerous occasions, Jack asked me to clarify what I meant and questioned if I truly believed that certain goals and timelines were realistic. Based on that questioning, I reassessed my action or decision and in some instances made changes. It also helped to hold me accountable to timelines upon which we had agreed and helped me measure and celebrate accomplishments along the way.

SUPPORT SYSTEMS

Achieving one's vision requires a support system in the same way that many plants require trellises, stakes, and other structures to support their growth. Had it not been for the tremendous support I was able to call upon as I pursued my vision of WUI, I doubt that I could have successfully launched that first program and built on that achievement. My network of friends and colleagues who saw and supported my vision was a key factor in my staying the course during difficult periods. In the early days of identifying organizations that might have an interest in supporting the WUI concept, my network provided access to potential corporate partners. It was also my network that helped design and develop many of the workshops that were offered in those early programs. They worked in a volunteer capacity to help me put the program together, especially in those early days when I was unable to compensate them in any way other than to buy an occasional dinner or give an occasional gift certificate as a thank-you.

In the very early days of WUI, Jack Yurish, his wife, Emma, and daughter, Anne, worked tirelessly as my volunteer support staff. Amy Gonzales and Susan Kendrick, WUI regional directors who had worked for me as training directors at NCR, volunteered their time and expertise to help develop and facilitate workshops. They traveled from the West Coast and Florida to help, and even stayed in my one-room apartment in those early days to help keep down costs.

Rosina Racioppi, president and chief operating officer of WUI, was employed by one of WUI's first corporate partners in New York. She was the human resources executive with Degussa Corporation and had served as a volunteer mentor for several years. When I persuaded Rosina to join me in January of 1998, to help expand and manage WUI programs, she took a significant decrease in salary to do so, but with total confidence that if she "loved what she did the money would follow."

My longtime friend and business colleague, Doris Hewkin, a former executive at Ralston Purina Company, volunteered her time and expertise to help create and manage budgets and was my accounts payable/receivable manager. She later became my official treasurer.

Nina Dougar, CPA, volunteered her time and expertise to manage the tax reporting process. Nina has recently joined WUI as chief financial officer. In addition, over the years, as other members of the WUI team have joined the group, they continue to support and enhance the overall vision.

Each one of the individuals who helped me establish WUI had an opportunity to add their input and today continues to have the opportunity to share their input, knowing that they are a part of this ongoing vision.

FLEXIBILITY AND ADAPTABILITY

It is important to remember that even with all the planning and actions identified, it is essential to be flexible and adaptable and remain committed to the overall vision. There were so many times over the years before the first corporate partners agreed to pilot the WUI program in New York that I had to reassess my original plans and make necessary changes. There were so many lessons learned along the way, including how much determination and resiliency mattered in the pursuit of a vision. One important lesson I learned was that not everyone had the same sense of urgency or vested interest in my vision as I did. I was willing to work around the clock in those early days and had to accept the fact that my passion for achieving results within the period I believed realistic was not necessarily how others viewed my timelines. Along with the sense of urgency and resilience, I had to hone my skills of patience, flexibility, and adaptability.

POSITIVE ATTITUDE

Winston Churchill, one of my personal heroes, said, "An optimist sees an opportunity in every calamity. A pessimist sees a calamity in every opportunity." In 1968, Dr. Spencer Silver, a

3M scientist, created glue with a low-grade stickiness, but did not have a use for it. Years later, 3M employee Art Fry wanted a bookmark that did not fall out of his hymnbook. Fry found an opportunity in what some considered a useless, disappointing invention when his bookmark need led him to Silver's adhesive—and, ultimately, to the development of the Post-it Note.

> "AN OPTIMIST SEES AN OPPORTUNITY IN EVERY CALAMITY. A PESSIMIST SEES A CALAMITY IN EVERY OPPORTUNITY."

Whenever I encountered a disappointment or a setback in those early days of my planning process, I reminded myself that throughout my life I not only survived but often thrived after meeting the challenges immediately following adverse situations.

It is important to assess setbacks as opportunities rather than roadblocks. They often result in better outcomes than were originally expected. For example, my original WUI planning process targeted the ideal number of program participants at 50. Three weeks before the first WUI program launched in New York City, on April 18, 1994, I was disappointed. I had 22 women registered for the program. However, the result of having only half of my intended number of participants was the creation of a far more personal learning environment. From that first group I learned it is essential to keep the number of participants below 35. Ten years later, this is still the ideal model for every program.

PERSISTENCE

There were many times during those early days of meeting with potential corporate partners, or people who might help me identify corporate partners, when I thought about giving up on my vision. In the winter of 1993-94, I rented a furnished one-room studio in New York City. My plan was to sell my home in Minnesota and buy another one in the New York City metro area once I saw that WUI was going to be successful. During that winter, New York experienced numerous snowstorms and other poor weather. The morning of one of my first information breakfast meetings, which I was hosting in the city, there was a paralyzing storm. In fact, the governor advised people to stay home.

I had guaranteed the hotel a minimum of 25 attendees and was clearly very nervous when only seven people managed to get there that morning. However, of those seven, four people at that meeting registered women for the very first program. The others asked me to meet with them and the decision makers in their organizations one-on-one. I then sent notes to everyone who had been unable to attend, letting them know I was going to reschedule a meeting. Almost every one of those original 25 invitees became corporate partners with WUI.

In the words of Joan Baez: "Action is the antidote to despair." There were so many times that I considered giving it all up and going back to the safety of my home in Minnesota, but there was always an inner voice keeping me going, and, of course, my wonderful cheering section. There is also one man to whom I will forever be grateful. A very successful head of a prestigious executive search firm in New York City advised me that WUI was a nice idea, but that "New York is a tough town to try and get this kind of a business going, especially for a woman." Although negative, his words motivated me. All a woman needs is someone to tell her she cannot, to know she can. I assure you that those words renewed my determination. They fueled my fire. In the words of Mary Kay Ash: "If you think you can, you will. If you think you can't, you're right."

"ACTION IS THE ANTIDOTE TO DESPAIR."

Leaders in an organization must stay the course and inspire others to achieve the organization's vision. Progress often depends on the people, the place, and the time being in alignment. The best idea, if sown on infertile ground, will sit there until the right conditions occur. The first stab at achieving a vision may not work. This does not mean that it will never work. It might just need some rain. The fact is that many visions become reality long after the seed is planted. Leonardo da Vinci imagined a "flying machine," but it wasn't until hundreds of years later that Wilbur and Orville Wright took that first flight at Kitty Hawk. It is never too late to act on an idea. Leonardo da Vinci may not have been able to make flight a reality, but the work he did and the drawings he made helped set it in motion.

Summary

Henry Ford said: "Coming together is a beginning, staying together is progress, and working together is success." In terms of vision, imagination and dreams are a beginning, action is progress, and ultimately creating a shared vision is success. The leader's ability to develop and create a shared vision is based upon:

- Imagination
- Clear communication
- Action
- Support systems
- Flexibility and adaptability
- Positive Attitude
- Persistence

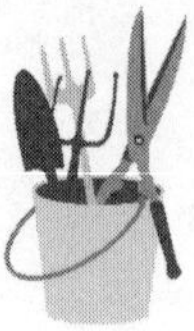

LEADERSHIP INVENTORY

1. Do you recognize and value the importance of and need for having a clearly defined personal and professional vision?

What is your vision?

Personal:

Professional:

What actions have you taken to define and pursue your vision?

How has this contributed to your growth and development?

What resources/activities help you to identify and implement the actions necessary to pursue and achieve your vision(s)?

When was the last time you used these resources to refine/implement your vision(s)?

2. Do you recognize and value the importance of and need for shared vision in organizational achievement?

What actions have you taken to define and pursue a shared vision?

How has this contributed to your growth and development?

How has this contributed to the growth and development of others?

How has this contributed to your organization's success?

What resources/activities help you to define and pursue a shared vision?

When was the last time you participated in an activity to define and pursue a shared vision?

3. There are several criteria identified in this chapter as being very important to creating a shared vision. Which criteria would you identify as your strengths?

Which criteria would you identify as areas of opportunity for improvement?

CALL TO ACTION

Based upon your response to the Leadership Inventory, identify three (3) actions to further your continuing development and success as a leader.

Action	Timetable
1.	
2.	
3.	

CHAPTER THREE

WHAT'S IN YOUR GARDEN SHED?

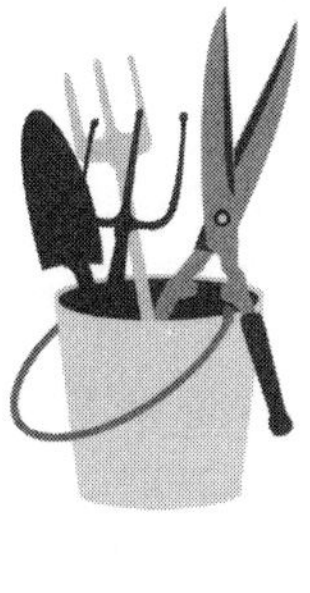

CHAPTER 3

WHAT'S IN YOUR GARDEN SHED?

> *"Intellectual honesty, the courage to look at things as they are, is the first test of mental maturity."*
>
> *—Edith Wharton*

Imagine a cherry tree growing in the corner of your yard. As the tree grows taller, it must be trimmed to promote outward growth. If it is a young sapling, trimming is easy. However, as it grows, trimming requires more work and time. A long-handled tree pruner offers gardeners the ability to reach to the top and trim even the most difficult branches, and requires less energy and lost time than climbing up and down a ladder to clip the out-of-reach sections.

Leaders, like highly skilled gardeners, need a variety of tools to be successful. In business, such tools offer leaders the opportunity to encourage growth and enhance productivity, while also helping to extend their reach and endurance. In Chapter 1, we identified the skills of successful leaders. Knowing which tool is appropriate for each skill and when to use it is key to both a gardener's and a leader's success.

Imagine going outside on a fall day, trying to rake a yard full of fallen leaves without a rake. You might be able to pick up a few leaves at a time with your hands, but as you work, more leaves would fall. Some individuals might be able to clear the yard with only their hands, but it would be a long, tiring process—one that could be accomplished faster, without the backache, if they knew which was the right tool for the job. As a skilled gardener knows that the rake is the appropriate tool to help clean up a yard, a leader knows that tools such as listening and negotiation are essential in helping to clear up problems in the workplace.

"WHEN WAS THE LAST TIME YOU ASSESSED YOUR LEADERSHIP TOOLS?"

Before I move forward, let me ask you one question: When was the last time you assessed your leadership tools? Before designing a garden or establishing a maintenance plan, gardeners and leaders have to look into their garden sheds to determine what tools they have, what condition they are in, and whether or not to replace old, worn-out tools. You might even need a trip to the garden center or hardware store to determine what new tools are available. In the chapters to follow, we will review the skills successful leaders require, the appropriate tools to use, when to use them, and how to maintain them.

I remember very clearly when I had to look into my garden shed—something Jack Yurish helped me do. In 1988, Jack was the executive vice president of NCR, one of NCR's new owners, and my manager. That year, he selected me to attend the

Experience Compression Laboratory (ECL), a weeklong leadership development program run by Barnum Associates International.

ECL requested the completion of an extensive assessment prior to attendance. The assessment required input from both workplace colleagues at different levels within the organization and personal friends. NCR had just been bought out and many of the new senior executives and peers doing the assessment had little or no prior interaction with me. I did not see their feedback until I attended ECL.

At my ECL session, there were 13 men and 2 women from around the world, meeting each other for the first time. We were asked to introduce ourselves by giving our first names and sharing something personal about ourselves. We were not allowed to mention anything about who we worked for or our titles. At a subsequent session, we were asked to select who we thought might be the best manager to work for, who we thought would be the worst manager, and who we would select as a social companion. I was selected by almost everyone for the latter. I did not receive any votes in the "good manager" category, but was ranked by a few as the worst manager to work for. Needless to say, I was disappointed with this feedback.

Next came the process of role-playing. We were interviewed for the roles of chief executive officer, chief operating officer, and lesser roles as well. Again, I was not selected for the most senior roles. This led to a very extensive one-on-one session with one of the ECL leaders regarding the feedback from my ECL colleagues and from my colleagues at NCR.

The feedback was very enlightening. It indicated that I was very highly ranked in leadership excellence by the individuals who reported to me, but was ranked very low by many of my peers and senior management. Only NCR's chief executive officer and my own manager, Jack, ranked me as having exceptional leadership skills. This session took place almost 15 years ago, when most senior leaders were men. The feedback, however, proved that the issue of my being a woman was not necessarily the reason I was not being viewed as a real player.

When I returned to work, I sat down with Jack to debrief. The ensuing conversation was one of the turning points in my career. It led me to be a proponent for the assessment process.

Through his years in the corporate world and his earlier experiences as an officer in the Marine Corps, Jack has had many opportunities to witness various styles of leadership and the factors that contribute to leadership success or failure. What Jack shared with me those 15 years ago is that all too often, especially at senior levels, failure occurs not because the person isn't intelligent or technically knowledgeable and competent but because they rigidly adhere to a certain leadership style, despite the fact that the style is inappropriate to the situation at hand or the relationship(s) in which they are engaged. People often ask Jack, "What is the best style to achieve success?" His answer usually is, "It depends on the situation being confronted." There is no one best style for handling all situations.

What Jack shared then still supports what current Catalyst studies report today: senior women rank style as the number two contributor to their success. They must have a style with which senior executives are comfortable. What I found was that my open, friendly, and often humorous style was getting in the way of my being perceived as a real player. I was perceived as a lightweight by those with very little knowledge of my competence. I remember Jack telling me that I was actually giving away my power when I did not read the room and adjust my style accordingly.

Karen Nemetz Duvall once worked for a manager who had a completely unflappable demeanor. "No matter what was happening, he was cool, calm and unemotional. He seemed like the perfect role model for executive presence, not a single crack under pressure," said Karen. "One night, we had a tragic fatality at our manufacturing plant. He was called in to handle the immediate aftermath, including internal and external communication. While he was crisp and efficient, he hardly seemed human. We wanted some evidence that he knew what we were thinking and feeling, and would respond as we needed. I've learned since then that you prepare yourself for a crisis every day of the year, by acknowledging, understanding and then managing human emotion." In life, especially in the business world, to be successful it is necessary to continuously adapt and adjust to our ever-changing environment.

"TO BE SUCCESSFUL, IT IS NECESSARY TO CONTINUOUSLY ADAPT AND ADJUST TO OUR EVER-CHANGING ENVIRONMENT."

LEADERSHIP STYLE

When Jack Yurish facilitates WUI workshops and consults with executives through his own company, he explains that leadership styles are categorized into different orientations, with a variety of labels being applied. "However," said Jack, "the styles usually revolve around some variant of four fundamental behavior patterns, described as the idealist, the doer, the analyzer, and the harmonizer." Jack explains that each orientation has its positive attributes as well as its excesses. "While each of us has a portion of each of these orientations within our leadership makeup, quite often, as a result of a person's life experiences, there's a tendency to rely heavily and primarily upon one of these orientations as our most preferred style and response. Some very satisfying results can occur if the situation at hand cries out for use of that particular orientation. On the other hand, less than desirable results and even disaster can occur, if it does not. Quite often, it is the inappropriate reliance on a single orientation and/or the excessive use of the positive attributes of that orientation that leads to difficulties in leadership attempts and interpersonal relationships. When people criticize us as being 'too this' or 'too that,' they are usually describing an excessive or ineffective use of what we might consider to be our primary strengths." The following are examples of what Jack describes:

PRIMARY ORIENTATIONS	SELF-PERCEPTIONS	OTHER'S PERCEPTIONS
Idealist	Principled Supportive	Impractical Overprotective
Doer	Action Oriented Forceful	Impulsive Domineering
Analyzer	Methodical Detail Oriented	Laborious Micromanager
Harmonizer	Tactful Adaptable	Political Wishy-Washy

The challenge and the opportunity for us, as leaders, is to enlarge our perspective of leadership situations and required leadership behaviors so that our own insight and capacity for responding is enhanced to the point where we are not locked in to a singular response to every situation. When we achieve this, we find, over time, our response to any situation will wind up on the side of the ledger labeled "effective performance" versus being on the side that is labeled "ineffective."

I refer to the ECL process and Jack's assessment as my "Outward Bound" program for discovering how others viewed me. Tennis star Billie Jean King said: "I think self-awareness is probably the most important thing towards being a champion." ECL and Jack offered me the opportunity to take inventory of myself and see myself from the outside in—how colleagues and senior management viewed me. As I mentioned previously, this

> "I THINK SELF-AWARENESS IS PROBABLY THE MOST IMPORTANT THING TOWARDS BEING A CHAMPION."

"inventory" made me a proponent of the assessment process. This process is the foundation of the WUI program today and something we stress as key to the participants' ongoing success. And quite frankly, a lot of this has to do with how people look, how people speak, how people listen, how people engage others. Those are all aspects of great leadership. For now, I'll discuss how people look. The rest will be covered in detail in the chapters that follow.

"THE LOOK"

I'd like to speak for a minute about this whole area of how people look. No matter what company you work in, whether it's a very casual-type company, say in the Silicon Valley area, versus a Wall Street-type company, where the style is much more traditional, there is absolutely a dress code. It may not be something that's written down; it may not be something that people think in this day and age is something they have to consider, but the fact is, yes, you do.

Every environment has its own code of behavior. If you're a savvy individual and you're working in a dress-down, casual type of environment, then you are probably not going to go in in a business suit with all of the accessories that you would use if you were making a call on a financial institution. But having said that, what I always tell people is: no matter what your environment is, take a look at what the top level of your organization looks like. What do they wear? How do they dress? What's their style? That's what you really need to be thinking about. And, as leaders, you should encourage employees to do the same.

> "EVERY DAY AT WORK IS A POTENTIAL JOB INTERVIEW."

Every day at work is a potential job interview. You have no idea who you'll meet—when you'll be in the elevator with senior executives. For all you know, you might be called into a meeting to do a presentation because your manager is sick. A client could make an unexpected visit on a "casual" Friday. Are you still looking "the part"? Are you wearing the type of outfit that you feel good about?

There is no question that how you look, how you present yourself, has everything to do with getting ahead in business. Now, some people have difficulty hearing that; but the truth is, it does count. Appearances do count. If you work in a casual, dress-down environment, make sure people always know you're the person who is always going to be in the really neat slacks and top and the really nice polished shoes. You are not there in tennis shoes. You are somebody who is admired because of the way that you present yourself.

INVENTORY ASSESSMENT

So, what is in your garden shed? Women who participate in the WUI programs are all assessed with Personnel Decisions International (PDI) Corporation's PROFILOR® multirater assessment tool. The assessments are conducted to help the participants discover not only their strengths, but also how to leverage them, and areas needing improvement. The assessments require participants and their management, peers, employees, and customers (when applicable) to rate participants on over 100 different areas. These include analyzing problems from different points of view, dealing constructively with failures and mistakes, establishing high standards of performance, living up to commitments, inspiring others to excel, making tough choices, and developing effective working relationships. From this feedback, the women are able to identify how they can build upon their strengths and decrease their weaknesses.

The first step in any improvement endeavor is usually some sort of inventory or status report. What do you know about your leadership orientation? What do you know about your tendencies? What are your leadership strengths? What are your excesses—things that prompt negative feedback from others?

What do you know about your most effective working environment? Your least effective? How can your supervisor most effectively manage you? How can others influence you? In addition to addressing these questions, if you have not previously taken any sort of leadership assessment, it would be helpful for you to seek out one or two of the more popular assessment tools. Information on appropriate assessments may be obtained from most human resource departments, college counselors, or industrial psychologists.

Rosina Racioppi has worked with thousands of WUI participants, their managers, and corporate partners in the assessment process. Through facilitating WUI assessment workshops, she has observed that there is often much anxiety regarding what the feedback will say about areas needing improvement. Participants want to know what they can fix so they can be perfect. The focus on perfection can be a major career inhibitor for many women, and contribute to their feelings of inadequacy and the "Imposter Syndrome."

WALLFLOWER OR SUNFLOWER?

The year I attended ECL, I also discovered the "Imposter Syndrome." In 1988 I was introduced to the book *If I'm So Successful, Why Do I Feel Like a Fake*, by Joan Harvey, Ph.D., and Cynthia Katz. It was the first time I recognized I was "suffering" from the Imposter Syndrome. When I read the book I found that, like many others, I really thought it was something only I felt—that no one else felt this way.

In the workshops that WUI conducts, we ask participants in the group if they can relate to the feeling of being an imposter. More than 70 percent put up their hands and then begin to talk about it. They are afraid of being exposed as a fraud, because they are afraid their achievements rest on factors other than their intelligence, creativity, hard work, and so on. Some believe it might have been luck or being in the right place at the right time. In other words, they believe they fooled people into overestimating their ability. Living with the doubt and the fear of being exposed could be a contributing factor to not taking a risk of going for something they could actually achieve. The individual is too afraid that he or she may not be successful—despite the fact they have already been able to accomplish major goals and contribute extremely well to business.

"TOO MANY PEOPLE OVERVALUE WHAT THEY ARE NOT AND UNDERVALUE WHAT THEY ARE."

I subscribe to the Malcolm Forbes quote: "Too many people overvalue what they are not and undervalue what they are." Following the suicide of her husband, Phil Graham, Katharine Graham took over as president of the Post Company. In her autobiography, *Personal History,* she wrote: "I never saw myself as 'taking over' anything or becoming the true head of the company. [...] While recognizing the importance of controlling the company, and having been willing to fight for it, I saw my job now as that of a silent partner, watching from the sideline as I tried to learn about the company to which I had tragically fallen heir. I saw myself as a bridge to my children and viewed my role before they could take over as supporting strong men [...] who were running things, and learning what I needed to do in case some big decisions came to me." At the time, Graham had no idea that the Pentagon Papers and Watergate sat poised on the horizon of United States history. Some might say that she was simply in the right place at the right time, but if she had remained a silent partner, would the Pentagon Papers have been published? Would the truth behind Watergate have been uncovered? Would *The Washington Post* be one of the nation's leading newspapers? Graham ascended to her position at *The Washington Post* in a time of turmoil—a period that could have been considered the right time or the wrong time, depending on how she approached the situation. In the end, she became known as the "Iron Lady" and one of the nation's most respected businesswomen.

Individuals experiencing the Imposter Syndrome are aware that they have certain abilities but do not view them as skills. They discount their abilities. In their eyes, their skills are all things that come naturally to them, so they take them for granted. I can relate to this on a personal level. For years I believed my ability to converse easily with others and have them open up to me was not a skill. My ability to bring people together to diffuse disharmony and work together to resolve problems was not anything special. Even when I started WUI, I spent months dismissing others' comments that this was a terrific forum and such a great idea. In fact, I think I used the term "this is not rocket science" to describe my bringing people together and giving them an opportunity to learn from each other. What is so tremendous about that? I wondered. Anybody can do this. And, of course, the fact is, when I look at it intellectually I can admit that not everybody does this, not everybody goes out and starts a nationwide program. This is a good example of dismissing and taking for granted a valuable skill.

One reason the Imposter Syndrome flourishes is due to the tendency to focus a great deal of energy on the things we do not do well, rather than on our strengths. For example, you may be terrific at speaking to large groups and motivating them with your words of wisdom, yet your writing skills may not be as great. You might worry extensively and needlessly about people discovering that you are not an equally good writer.

Of course, one of the greatest fears of people who suffer from this Imposter Syndrome is the fear of failing. Anything short of perfect brings out self-doubt. So in order to be seen as significant, the person holds himself or herself to a standard that does not allow for mistakes. The shame and embarrassment of failing or having other people see them fail is something that many people who suffer from this syndrome truly fear.

When a project has been successfully completed, such individuals will discount the opinions and comments of those who think they have done extremely well and instead focus on the comment of someone who does not necessarily share that belief. If 20 people indicate the person has done well, but only one person has one or two forms of criticism, the latter is whom the Imposter Syndrome sufferer focuses on. I can remember giving speeches and being involved in workshops where there were evaluations. No matter how many evaluations rated me as a 5 on a scale of 1 to 5, I would always look for the ones that ranked me as a 3 and immediately think, "Uh-oh, obviously I am not good. I am not delivering the type of speech or information to people that I should have been doing." Any such rating would immediately trigger my self-doubts and played beautifully into my whole feeling of being an imposter.

In one of the WUI workshops, there was a huge gasp when a woman with a Ph.D., whose demeanor and appearance was that of the executive-type woman, raised her hand as suffering from Imposter Syndrome. When I asked her why she felt she was such an imposter she immediately looked at her team and said: "I have nowhere near the expertise in the corporate world and management that my peers have." Her peers looked at her in disbelief and said, "But you've got a Ph.D. We're in awe of *you*."

"THE FIRST PROBLEM FOR ALL OF US, MEN AND WOMEN, IS NOT TO LEARN, BUT TO UNLEARN."

Gloria Steinem once said: "The first problem for all of us, men and women, is not to learn, but to unlearn." The first step to really coming to grips with the Imposter Syndrome and making positive movement in the direction of overcoming it is to really acknowledge (a) that you are not alone in this belief and

(b) that it is quite frankly successful people who suffer from this. It is also something that, once recognized and once understood, many people can rationally deal with. One of my recommendations is to take the time to acknowledge all of the accomplishments you have had in life. When doing assessments, focus on the strengths and not the weaknesses. As Gail Sheehy said: "Self-esteem isn't everything; it's just that there's nothing without it."

When I talk with many of the WUI groups, the conversation often turns to the lack of confidence that some of the women feel when they are going to face a stressful situation; in particular, the number one fear is that of making a speech in front of a large group. There is data indicating that fear of death ranks below fear of public speaking, so when people say they would rather die than speak in public, they aren't joking.

My response to women asking how to overcome fear is: underwear. Underwear can change your life. As Lawrence Ferlinghetti wrote in his poem "Underwear": ". . . we all have to deal with [it]. Everyone wears some kind of underwear." It provokes a lot of laughter when I ask women if they remember being told by their mothers never to go anywhere with holes in their underwear in case they were in an accident. My point, however, is that when you wear something you love and it makes you feel good, you will boost your confidence. So don't listen to those who look down on spending time on how you look and what you wear. If it makes you feel good, go for it.

> "UNDERWEAR CAN CHANGE YOUR LIFE."

Play to Your Strengths

Rosina Racioppi advises WUI participants to play to their strengths. What are your core competencies? This may be difficult for some to consider (we are much better at listing what we do not do well). Start by listing your key accomplishments and how you were able to achieve them. What skills/competencies do you possess that allowed you to achieve this success?

My recommendation to the women who go through the WUI program is to take the time to sit down and look at and document in a journal all those moments of achievement—from as far back as they can remember, everything from the first time their kindergarten teacher displayed their artwork to the first "A" they received to recent business accomplishments. Engage family members, friends, and colleagues in this experiment and ask them what they remember about you and to point out an accomplishment. I know this has helped me and I encourage all of you to do the same thing. And on those days when you think, "I am not going to be able to pull this off, people are going to see that I am not capable," review your journal and your list of accomplishments. It will give you all the confidence and courage to move forward with the belief that yes, you can. It will help remind you of your strengths and how to play to them.

Part of playing to your strengths and increasing other's support of what you are trying to accomplish is letting others know what you are doing. One of the biggest mistakes successful women make is to sit and wait to be noticed. We have all heard the saying "It is not what you know, it is who you know that counts." My "Otte Thotte" and caveat to others is: "It is not what you know, it's who knows you know." Mike Addington is the director of human resources, diversity succession planning, and specialized recruitment at John Deere. Mike's advice is: "If it's gonna happen, only you can make it happen." According to Mike, "The people that perform the best and provide the most value will show up on the radar screen." Showing the desire to learn, build skills, and develop competencies, and continuing to develop yourself, is important. While you cannot forget your areas in need of improvement, by playing to your strengths, you offer yourself additional opportunities to "flex" those strengths in the eyes of others. The support of others for your areas of strength often translates into support for developing additional strengths.

"IT'S NOT WHAT YOU KNOW, IT'S WHO KNOWS YOU KNOW."

AVOID PERFECTIONISM

How many of us, when reviewing the results of 360 assessments, immediately look at all competencies on which we were rated lowest, and use those lowest rankings to establish our development plan? This assumes that we need to fix ourselves so we can be perfect! WUI sees the women in our programs struggling with this when they are reviewing their feedback. Rosina Racioppi reminds participants: "Perfectionism is a career-limiting strategy. It also dilutes your focus from your key strengths." Karen Nemetz Duvall adds: "If there has been one area I struggle with the most, it has been how to teach new leaders to effectively use their time. Each of us processes and acts on information in our own unique style. However, many who have persistent problems with time management do not understand what's most important, insist on 100 percent when 80 percent will do, need to know everything, or aren't able to delegate effectively. It is critical that leaders have the extra capacity to think, explore, and communicate informally."

Part of falling into the perfectionism trap is wasting time and energy on doing 100 percent when only 80 percent is required. For example, when developing a chart for a presentation, all that is usually needed are the facts and a nice presentation. "Nice" requires a clean, organized, sharp presentation. It does not necessarily require color graphics and animation. Going the extra mile is always appreciated, but when coupled with perfectionism, it can result in too much time spent in one area, leaving less time to develop other areas. Develop a realistic goal for yourself and use your energy to identify your key strengths and build on them. Try to maintain a level of organizational savvy to avoid wasting time.

ORGANIZATIONAL SAVVY

When I ask WUI participants what "organizational savvy" means to them, the response is usually along the lines of "knowing what to do before you even have to know what to do." It is what I refer to as "guttuitiveness"—simply having the ability to read between the lines, listening for what is really being said, and knowing the right thing to say at the right time. When I discuss this particular subject I ask if being a savvy individual is a positive thing. And almost always, the answer is yes. I ask participants to think about people in their own organization who they can just look at and know are what we call savvy individuals. When I ask them to describe these people, their descriptions are usually that they

> "ORGANIZATONAL SAVVY IS LIKE HAVING A COMMAND OF A NATIVE LANGUAGE."

have a presence and the ability not only to get things done but also to get things done well.

I will also ask the same groups if there is another word that comes to mind when I refer to being organizationally savvy. Invariably, the answer is yes: being political. When I ask them if that is a positive statement, the answer is no. Nobody likes to be thought of as being political or to be referred to as a political animal. And the difference is that being political has a negative connotation because everybody thinks of the Eddie Haskells of the world—Eddie Haskell of *Leave It to Beaver*, who was simply what everybody thought of as a kiss up. And people who simply kiss up for their own well-being, for what they want to get out of something, are not organizationally savvy people. They are people who are doing it as a means to an end to benefit only themselves. Organizationally savvy people, however, are people who want to get things done for others, with others, and for the good of the entire company. They are people who want the opportunity to contribute their best effort to get the best results possible. I am sure that as you read this, you can visualize a political person and someone who is organizationally savvy and you can see the difference. How do people view you in this area?

Karen Nemetz Duvall has said that organizational savvy is like "having a command of a native language. Once you know the language, it's important to share it. I debrief with my team after every significant political interaction. Sometimes this saves a bright person from crashing and burning, but more often, it raises his level of participation and influence in the organizational fray. People need to step out to get things done, but they need the confidence of organizational insight first." After receiving my assessment feedback from ECL, I realized I was not as savvy as I needed to be when interacting with others. It was at this point that I had to put together an effective development plan for myself.

DEVELOPMENT PLAN

After reflecting upon my ECL-related feedback, and with Jack Yurish's guidance, I set about putting together a plan to transfer my learnings from the assessment process into making the change that was clearly necessary for me to be viewed as a major contributor to the organization. As with vision, identifying what needs to be done is not enough. As a part of the development plan, WUI participants are required to incorporate the means to measure their improvement. Although the core remains the same, the plans evolve to address the different points participants reach.

Rosina Racioppi has noted that creating development plans, or garden shed maintenance schedules, has become a ritual in many corporations. Unfortunately, such plans are usually linked to a performance review process and rarely are used after the process is completed. The plans are filed and stuck in a drawer until the following year. Gardens left unattended for too long become overgrown with weeds.

"BRING THE PLAN OUT OF THE DRAWER."

Leadership development and growth is like gardening—an enriching lifetime endeavor requiring constant care.

Rosina challenges WUI participants to "bring the plan out of the drawer" and keep it alive during the year. "The challenge for managers and employees," says Rosina, "is to create development plans that will influence an individual's career growth and will be used actively during the year. Many of the women who have participated in our programs tell us how they complete a development plan every year at work, yet through participating in our programs have learned how to make their plans come to life."

In its book *Development FIRST*, written by David Peterson and Mary Dee Hicks, PDI established and defined the first five steps, listed below, to help individuals proactively drive development and establish a cycle of continuous learning. WUI promotes these steps to participants, explaining that the steps often repeat themselves and/or occur in different order. For example, reflection and seeking feedback occur repeatedly throughout the self-assessment process.

Development FIRST **Model:***

Focus on priorities: Identify your critical issues and goals.

Implement something every day: Stretch your comfort zone daily.

Reflect on what happens: Extract maximum learning from your experiences.

Seek feedback and support: Learn from others' ideas and perspectives.

Transfer learning into next steps: Adapt and plan for continued learning.

Sample Development Plan Adapted from *Development FIRST*:*

Step 1	Step 2	Step 3	Step 4
STRENGTH TARGETED	**ACTION PLAN**	**INVOLVEMENT OF OTHERS**	**TARGET DATE**
STRENGTH: Coach and Develop	1. Volunteer to be trained as an assessor for in-house development centers.	boss	7/1
OBJECTIVE: • Increase my skill for identifying strengths and development needs	2. Participate in training for assessment.	assessment staff	8/15
	3. Serve as an assessor in two centers.	boss	Sept.-Dec.
	4. Use assessment skills with my own staff for career development discussions.	staff	Nov.-Dec.

*Reprinted with permission from *Development FIRST.*
Copyright © 1997, Personnel Decisions International Corporation. All Rights Reserved.

FOCUS ON PRIORITIES

Not everything can be urgent and not everything can be important. In the scheme of all that has to be done, three or four things that rise to the top are of primary importance. Where do you want to be in the next two years? In five years? Knowing the direction you want to take your career brings clarity to your development plan. It enables you to determine the two or three key competencies you may need to focus on and what resources you may need to achieve your goals. Some abdicate control over their career to their manager or company. When this happens, you can end up in jobs that you do not enjoy, but that someone else thought would be good for you. Getting your career goals in focus provides you with more control over your career.

Retired IBM executive Debbie Murphy often took risks in setting priorities around the workload and trying not to get caught up in the "I have to get it all done" trap. "Today, we can no longer be perfectionists in dotting every i and crossing every t," said Debbie. "Companies need productive, healthy employees to ensure the strongest workforce, and people who believe they can only be successful by working 24 hours a day, 7 days a week, will not be productive and successful in the long term. I challenged myself and my staff to prioritize the most critical work items and then proactively reviewed these priorities with the key stakeholders to ensure the right expectations are set. I also made sure to include things that give me personal satisfaction like mentoring employees or participating in diversity council activities. I unhooked from my business life by trying not to work on weekends or while on vacation so I could clear my mind, which made me a more productive contributor. I always said I had a life outside of work, and I am proud of it." By "unhooking" herself from work, Debbie gave herself the ability to reflect. This does not mean spend your out-of-office time with you head in the office. You have to unplug from the office to clear your head before going back into the office and reflecting on your progress.

REFLECT

Edith Wharton once said: "Intellectual honesty, the courage to look at things as they are, is the first test of mental maturity." When reflecting on the contents in your garden shed, you have to be honest with yourself, and willing to take input from others about how they view your strengths and areas of opportunity for improvement. This input should come from individuals who respect you, as well as those who do not. Asking for help is one step in reflection. Before starting a project, you have to reflect on your first step. You also have to periodically reflect throughout the project, asking yourself if you are on course and satisfied with your progress. Perhaps you want more, perhaps you are overwhelmed and want less. The ECL process and the feedback I received from Jack Yurish offered the opportunity to reflect upon critical issues, how those issues were a roadblock for me, and what I needed to do to assess those issues.

"INTELLECTUAL HONESTY, THE COURAGE TO LOOK AT THINGS AS THEY ARE, IS THE FIRST TEST OF MENTAL MATURITY."

Implement Your Plan

Once you have identified the key areas of your development, find opportunities within your current job where you can work toward your goal. For me, the first step was to find out why people thought the way they did about me. I requested time with each of my peers and senior executives who had completed my assessment. I asked if I could discuss my learnings and asked them for clarification on why they had ranked me as they did. I also asked for time with those who had not completed the assessment.

Feedback

Sometimes we can learn much more about ourselves and how others perceive us through feedback from people who have the least admiration for us. You need to be prepared to take all of the input you receive in a positive manner. Avoid being defensive and trying to convince anyone who gives unwelcome feedback that they are wrong.

When I requested time to talk to the senior executives and my peers about my assessment, I had to listen as they shared their input and I had to remember not to attempt to challenge what I thought was their mistaken perception of me. I asked them to share examples with me. But most important, I asked them for their help.

Understand that others' perceptions of you are their reality. No matter how much you try to justify why they should not think or feel or see you the way they do, the fact is that they do see you the way in which they are describing you, and you need to think about how you can improve that situation.

> "OTHERS' PERCEPTIONS OF YOU ARE THEIR REALITY."

Understand the strengths and the weaknesses of what you bring to the organization and how they play into what you truly want to do. Michele Coleman Mayes advises others: "Be yourself. It might take awhile to find out what that means, but do not ever be afraid to search." The key is being able to change yourself while still being you.

As I met with each person at NCR, I asked what I could do to improve what they perceived to be an area of concern, and asked if they would, from time to time, agree to give me feedback on my progress. I regularly asked Jack Yurish and other key executives to debrief me after key meetings, and I asked for feedback on what they thought I had done well and what could be improved.

When I was in meetings, I refrained from my usual upbeat bantering and other pleasantries and set about presenting my requirements or recommendations in a very straightforward, businesslike manner. I quickly began to see executives and peers respond much more positively. One example of how this experience resulted in a successful outcome was when one of the key executives who had ranked me very low in leadership ability requested that I begin meeting with his sales executives and their major accounts to establish ongoing account management and support.

Within 18 months of the ECL assessment I was promoted, becoming the first corporate female vice president and officer of NCR. I am not going to lie and say that as a result of this experience everyone gained a higher respect for my abilities. But it most certainly improved perceptions of me to a great degree among a number of my colleagues, who consequently had a higher regard and respect for my abilities.

It is also important to note that the tool I took for granted as I struggled with the Imposter Syndrome—that of being a terrific communicator—is what pulled me through in the end. I knew I had the ability to communicate, but Jack had pointed out that my style was holding me back. By reflecting, playing to my strengths, developing a plan, and taking action, I changed the course of my career and established stronger relationships with those who had originally doubted my abilities.

MAINTENANCE

Development plans should be fluid documents that are reviewed continuously. The plans must continue to evolve as we evolve, promoting lifelong learning and development. As Carly Fiorina said: "One of the things that distinguishes success from mediocrity or failure is the ability to keep learning. . . . You can learn from everything that happens in life and from everyone you come in contact with in life. I hope I've taken advantage of all those events and all those people. And I hope I've gotten better and more effective every year."

I have never met a truly outstanding leader who did not value and pursue continuous learning. They are current on world and business issues, they participate in ongoing professional development programs, they are involved with external organizations that allow them to continue to hone their leadership skills. These leaders know that they must regularly assess their strengths and areas for improvement and be willing to make whatever necessary changes need to be made.

As I said earlier, the key to a gardener's and leader's success is knowing the right tools and knowing how and when to use and update them. For example, one can acquire a garden shovel at a gardening center or hardware store just as one can acquire an MBA from a university. If one does not know when it is appropriate to use or update a certain tool (or apply the knowledge gained through an MBA program), the desired results will take longer to be achieved or not be achieved at all.

With the complexity of today's world, no one person or one leadership style can satisfy all the demands for effective leadership. Different situations call for different orientations and strengths. The truly effective leader realizes this fact and has a very clear picture as to what skills, abilities, and orientation they bring to the game. Recognizing this, they then make every effort to surround themselves with individuals who can help them extend and supplement these skills and abilities so that the inclusive use of all the diverse strengths available in any situation are put to work for optimum achievement and the benefit of the common good.

Once you have assessed what tools are in your garden shed, and updated its inventory, it is time to start assessing the environment in which you work or will be working.

SUMMARY

To continue their development as leaders, individuals must:

- CONDUCT SKILL ASSESSMENTS
- INVITE FEEDBACK
- ESTABLISH AND IMPLEMENT DEVELOPMENT PLANS
- PLAY TO THEIR STRENGTHS
- AVOID PERFECTIONISM
- UNDERSTAND THE IMPORTANCE OF BEING ORGANIZATIONALLY SAVVY
- FOCUS ON PRIORITIES

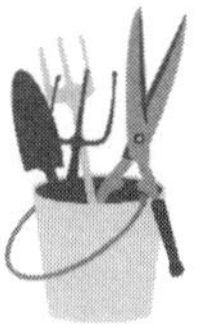

Leadership Inventory

1. Do you recognize and value the importance of and need for ongoing skill assessments?

What actions have you taken to assess your skills?

How has this contributed to your growth and development?

How has this contributed to your organization's success?

What resources/activities help you to engage in the process of skill assessment?

When was the last time you used these resources/activities in pursuit of this goal?

2. Do you recognize and value the importance of and need for a documented development plan?

What actions have you taken to develop a plan?

How has this contributed to your growth and development?

How has this contributed to your organization's success?

What resources/activities help you in documenting, modifying, and updating your plan?

When was the last time you used these resources and updated your plan?

3. Do you recognize and value the importance of and need for situational leadership (knowing which skills and behaviors are appropriate and effective in any situation) in achieving leadership excellence and organizational success?

What actions have you taken to demonstrate situational leadership?

How has this contributed to your growth and development?

How has this contributed to the growth and development of others?

How has this contributed to your organization's success?

What resources/activities help you to assess situational leadership requirements?

When was the last time you used these resources and/or applied situational leadership skills to achieve significant organizational success?

CALL TO ACTION

Based upon your response to the Leadership Inventory, identify three (3) actions to further your continuing development and success as a leader.

Action	Timetable
1.	
2.	
3.	

SECTION II

CREATING THE ENVIRONMENT

CHAPTER FOUR

ASSESSING THE ENVIRONMENT

CHAPTER 4

ASSESSING THE ENVIRONMENT

> *"All gardeners live in beautiful places because they make them so."*
>
> *—Joseph Joubert*

How does your garden grow? In order to grow, people, like plants, need to be in an environment that fosters their own individual needs and supports their desire to grow and achieve their potential. Rosie the Riveter joined the workforce beginning in 1942. During WWII, women were needed in the workforce. The environment was right for such a change. Following the war, when the men returned to the workforce, many of the "Rosies" returned home. It took some time for the social mores to swing back in Rosie's favor, but it was a new environment that first welcomed her, and a changing environment, fed by initiatives such as the Equal Rights Amendment and Title IX, that offered future generations of "Rosies" a permanent place. A lot has changed, with more women in permanent positions of responsibility. One thing that has not changed is the role the environment plays in an individual's success.

Through my years of working for major corporations, being a wife and mother and starting my own company, I experienced firsthand how important the environments of these situations are to my continuing growth and success, and ultimately my feelings of personal fulfillment.

I was educated in England at an all-girls school in the 1950s. The prevailing thought at the time was that young women should become wives and mothers. If a young woman was not "selected" for that role or did not choose to do that at the age of 18, she was encouraged to become a secretary, nurse, librarian, or—the number one most acceptable and somewhat prestigious career—a teacher. It was the latter that my teacher and my father encouraged me to consider when it became apparent that I was a somewhat independent young woman with a desire to do something more than become a wife and mother at a young age.

I followed their advice and pursued a career in teaching. However, one of many life-altering events occurred during this time, and resulted in my following a very different path. My father died suddenly. Although it was a tremendously sad and difficult time for my family, it resulted in my looking at who I really wanted to be.

Ever since I was a child, my life had been one of continuous change and relocation due to the war years and my father's company sending us to different locations throughout England and Wales. I had become very comfortable with this lifestyle and enjoyed the adventure of it all. When a wonderful opportunity presented itself for me to go to the United States—the land of opportunity—I took it. The United States proved to be the environment in which I would thrive.

In recent years, while discussing career choices with women who are not passionate about their careers, I am often told that they would have preferred to do something different with their lives, but for various reasons chose otherwise. I have seen many individuals who simply did not thrive, even though they had the skills and desires. They had become plants that, simply put, did not grow. They languished, never fully achieving their potential. When assessing the environment, they did not first assess their needs. For example, I have seen some of the greatest field salespeople being rewarded for their efforts by being promoted to sales managers, directors, and vice presidents. Although the promotions are appreciated, this often results in such individuals not being the best leaders; they thrive better in their field sales environment than in the corporate headquarters.

Years ago my husband and I bought a home in Minnesota and fell in love with its truly lovely backyard. It was filled with wonderful old oaks, maple trees, and evergreens, giving the feeling of a miniature forest. Similar to the sales representatives taking that corporate promotion, we did not consider what that landscape brought with it—that it was not conducive for the flower beds we wanted and that it required a great deal of maintenance in the fall as the leaves fell.

I have friends who prefer less labor-demanding yards. For example, it would not be in their best interest or conducive to their particular orientation to take on a garden requiring a major commitment to seeding, fertilizing, pruning, and weeding. Their lives would be happier had they chosen or created an environment requiring very little maintenance. In the workplace, leaders need to fully recognize that the environment they create will play a major role in their ultimate satisfaction and success, and that of those they are planning to "grow." Part of assessing the environment is making a checklist of what your ideal environment should have. You need this in order to know what to assess.

DETERMINE THE RIGHT ENVIRONMENT

Before accepting her current position as a vice president at the Walt Disney Company, Betsy Wanner launched a career search rooted in finding her most desirable work environment. With 23 years in financial services, Betsy was ready for a change. As she began to assess her needs and develop a checklist, she saw that she knew more about what she did not want rather than what she did. "Plan A" involved thinking through possible job moves within her current place of employment. However, after much consideration, Betsy determined that she needed to look outside the organization.

Betsy began to reassess the situation. Taking time to figure out what was important to her was critical before moving to anything new. "'Plan B' was more extreme, but proved to be the right move," said Betsy. "I made the choice to leave my job and work a plan that included personal time to decompress, time to figure out the right next step, and then an actual job search. The sense of control, empowerment, and freedom that followed only validated my decision. It was clearly time to move on; I just needed to figure out where."

As a vice president in financial services, Betsy's expertise and strategic and business skills were transferable. "The challenge was to maintain an executive level in a new industry that would incorporate my newly identified needs and values: creativity, imagination, inspiration, belief in and respect for the product or service," said Betsy.

"VALUES, CORE NEEDS, BOUNDARIES, AND **CHOICE** TOOK ON NEW MEANINGS."

Using resources like executive coaching and job search tools, the process of determining her next career choice turned into a process of understanding "who I am" rather than deciding specific interests. For Betsy, words such as *values, core needs, boundaries*, and *choice* took on new meanings. Outlining what each meant to her created her "own definition of success and a personal map to achieve it." When she was ready to start a job search, the map became a "professional barometer." In the past, she asked questions such as: Can I do this job? How do I sell myself? For this job search, she asked: Do I want this job? Does it meet my core needs? Are the values of the company aligned with mine? Asking a hiring manager questions about the organization's criteria for success, company culture, decision-making methods, and employee retention were just as important as asking about the job responsibilities.

Now a vice president at the Walt Disney Company, Betsy's job search ended in her finding an environment in which she could thrive while nurturing the growth of the organization and its employees. For others like Betsy, who are considering new careers outside their current organizations or industries, it is important to do the homework and determine the organization's environment.

> "METHODS OF RECOGNITION SAY A LOT ABOUT THE ORGANIZATION."

You may want to ask such questions as: Are women and minorities valued? What initiatives are in place to recruit and retain women and minorities? If you value security above all else, check out what reorganizations and layoffs have occurred and ask how they are handled. Are layoffs determined by a last-in first-out policy?

If a benefits package including ongoing educational development is a necessity, ask what is available. Does the organization offer its own professional development programs?

If you thrive in environments that recognize and reward creativity rather than strictly sales, ask about the organization's recognition and reward process. Methods of recognition say a lot about the organization. Does it offer large bonuses for increased sales efforts and smaller bonuses (or none at all) for process improvements or innovation?

If the move you are considering is internal, talk with different levels of employees within the division you are considering. Do the same homework you would if you were considering an outside organization. The following are some measurements you might use to determine the right environment.

Organization Measurements:

- Listed in *Fortune*'s 100 Best Companies to Work For
- Awards for employee/customer satisfaction (i.e., Baldrige, Catalyst, YWCA)
- Employee climate surveys conducted by external source
- Low employee-turnover statistics
- Continuing-education benefits
- Ongoing internal/external professional development programs
- Succession-planning process required for all management
- Management compensation tied to employee/customer satisfaction data
- 360-degree assessment process used to determine employees' strengths and areas of opportunity for development
- Mentoring/coaching process in place

Division/Department Measurements:

- Consistent, ongoing one-on-one and team feedback sessions with employees
- Employee turnover/retention/promotion statistics
- Customer feedback statistics
- Productivity statistics

- Division/department performance against quality standards, organization requirements, cost containment, budgets
- Commitment to employee development through internal/external programs
- Recognition process utilized
- Department's or division's ability to attract/retain achievement-oriented individuals.

BALANCE

One of the key things to assess about an environment is whether it will support your needs for a balanced life. Even if you are fortunate enough to be in the highest paid or most exciting and rewarding career, without balance in your life, it will lead to stress and burnout, and dissatisfaction with all areas of your life.

As the facilitator of WUI's Achieving Balance: Managing at the Speed of Life workshop, WUI regional director Susan Kendrick has helped thousands of women to understand the key learning points of balance. The main points Susan highlights are:

- Know that balance is not a destination
- Understand what your true values are
- Make choices that support your values
- Set your boundaries
- Zap the tolerations
- Balance is like art

KNOW THAT BALANCE IS NOT A DESTINATION. It is not some place where you will "arrive" one day. I sometimes hear people say, "Someday, I am going to be balanced." Balance shouldn't be looked at as a goal: Balance is a way of life. Celebrities and business leaders such as Ann Fudge, chairman and CEO of Young & Rubicam, who took a two-year sabbatical after leaving her previous company, are making headlines for taking time off. What a great example of a senior executive taking a "time out" that did not adversely affect her career.

> "BALANCE SHOULDN'T BE LOOKED AT AS A GOAL: BALANCE IS A WAY OF LIFE."

UNDERSTAND WHAT YOUR TRUE VALUES ARE. In order to feel that you are achieving balance, you must have a clear idea of what's really important to you, what you *really* value. There seems to be a correlation between people who have faced serious loss and those that know what is truly important in their life. When faced with crisis, a serious loss, or lifestyle change, people quickly know what they value most. *Values are the absolutes for balance to happen.* "Armed with the knowledge that I wanted to be 'an independent businesswoman' and live in the Southwest, I moved from the Midwest to Phoenix and happily accepted my first job," said Betsy Wanner. "That step unknowingly launched a 23-year career in financial services based on little more than geography and the fact that I had to support myself in a respectable way. Based on that criteria, it's little wonder that my professional life eventually became frustrating.

Years had been spent adapting to the needs of the job and company with little thought to my own values or interests, and my identity was becoming inextricably tied to my work. The hours spent to get ahead, and the hours required once you do, leave little time to pursue interests outside of work. I learned to be a 'thinker' instead of my natural 'feeler' personality, learned to think about today instead of tomorrow. My professional skills became my personal approach: wedding announcements and party invitations read like business memos; I had more dinner dates and took more exotic trips with colleagues than with my husband or friends outside of the company. While I had achieved success by the usual measures (money, title at a Fortune 100 company, 'cookware' instead of 'pots and pans,' a professional 'walker' for my dog), I was also tired, bored, and dissatisfied." As discussed in the section "Determine the Right Environment," Betsy was ready for a change. What was important had shifted. She knew that she wanted more than "geography" and the ability to support herself. She wanted to work with an organization that had the same values she had. "'Falling into' an industry and working with great companies during the first half of my career, I learned," said Betsy. "'Choosing' an industry based on values and working with a great company during the last half of my career, I enjoy."

MAKE CHOICES THAT SUPPORT YOUR VALUES. Every day we are faced with a multitude of decisions. Should I take the volunteer position that is open? Should I stay a little late to work through this stack of files? Each time you are faced with a decision, ask yourself, How does this serve my values? A colleague of mine who had two small children told me that she was up for a promotion. She was very flattered by the fact that she was regarded as having high potential at her company. Yet she felt torn. What she valued the most was her family, and lately work was all-consuming. She was giving her family—those who she valued *the* most—the "leftovers." The choice she had was tough, but when she reviewed her life values, the answer was clear, and she knew that while the promotion and all the trappings would be great, it would also require a trade-off of even less family time. She made the decision, tough as it was, to pass up the offer.

Set your boundaries. Draw a line in the sand. That is a great visual for defining your boundaries. Keep in mind that when you hear yourself saying, "I can't," it means one of two things: you don't know how or you choose not to. The truth sometimes hurts, but when you hear yourself saying, "I can't leave before six!" you are really saying, "I choose not to." Tough as it is to face, we often make choices that sabotage our own values, which, in turn, make balance impossible. Marisa, a director at a large company, told Susan that she was excited about her new role as manager, and in starting anew she wanted to start positive balance habits. One of them was to leave the office at 6 P.M. Yet day after day, she was still at her desk hours after 6 P.M. had passed. That is because she hadn't firmly established her boundaries, which support her values of family.

Values are the boss of boundaries. People with clear values also have very clear boundaries. Maryann King MacIntyre, vice president and team leader, cash management, for Citizens Bank of Massachusetts, had to make a choice between work and family. "As my children arrived and it became necessary to balance work and family, my priority was always family. However, as an aspiring professional, I was aware of my working obligations and the related advancements thereof," said Maryann. "One effective tool for me has been a 6 A.M. to 4 P.M. work schedule that was consistently maintained. At the same time, I let it be known, when warranted, I would stay past 4 P.M. to get the job done. My career has flourished and we have a near-perfect record of sit-down family dinners, along with school plays and concerts. It was important to set time boundaries around my professional commitment. These boundaries helped my peers and superiors plan accordingly. Our deliverables were always met."

ZAP THE TOLERATIONS. Think about what it's like when you have a small pebble in your shoe. It's an aggravating feeling that doesn't initially keep you from moving forward, but it sure is grating on your nerves, and eventually you can't stand it any longer. Tolerations are like that. They zap us of the positive energy that's so critical to finding balance. Tolerations can be as simple as the piles of documents sitting on your desk week after week, or more serious, like putting up with inappropriate comments or treatment from others. There are two things you can do about tolerations: reframe them or respond to them. To reframe toleration, you look at it from a different point of view. For example, you can decide that in the scheme of things the piles on your desk just aren't worth stressing over. Or you can respond to them, meaning you will take action to get the files off your desk so it no longer causes you stress and imbalance.

"Balance is like art. Great art looks different to every person, just as balance looks different for each of us."

Balance is like art. Great art looks different to every person, just as balance looks different for each of us. Rather than compare your life to those around you, think about what balance in *your* life would look like. Susan asks participants to imagine themselves at their eightieth birthday party. Friends and family are all around, smiling and celebrating your life. What do you want them saying about you? What contributions and accomplishments do you want to be sure have happened?

Assessing the Elements

After deciding what kind of environment will support their vision, gardeners have to assess the existing environment to evaluate whether it meets their needs. This includes assessing both the elements and what is currently growing.

When gardeners decide to design a new landscape or garden, they have to recognize the elements affecting the environment. Geographic locations, weather patterns, and soil content must be considered before gardeners can determine if their vision of the garden is achievable. For example, I have often admired many of the beautiful plants in my friend Val's garden in England. I have to accept the fact that in my home in New Jersey, however, it is impossible for some of those plants to thrive or survive.

In business, conducting due diligence with senior executives, customers, suppliers, and current employees will provide leaders with what is needed to assess "the elements." "The gardener does not make the garden; the garden makes the gardener," is an anonymous quote that was sent to me by a colleague. The environment of that garden will determine how it is gardened. In business, a leader may enter a new organization with the ability to lead, but how they lead is determined by the organization's environment. Is it a healthy, productive environment or, as in a garden to be cleared, are there rocks; does the soil need adjusting; or is there a sprinkler system in need of repair? For example, "Once you have the lay of the land, you can then determine what actions need to be taken to build a great team," said Sandy Beach Lin. "This can include team building, retreats, one-on-one meetings with the team members to solicit their ideas, and yes, when necessary, removal of individuals who choose not to pursue the chosen strategy with you."

> "THE GARDENER DOES NOT MAKE THE GARDEN; THE GARDEN MAKES THE GARDENER."

During one of the NCR buyouts, the new leadership met with each department manager individually to ask about the organization and the individual's role within the organization. The leadership evaluated the elements affecting the environment, as well as what the current environment was growing, through observation, asking questions, and listening to the answers. This helped them determine what needed to be done in order to move forward. The leadership had to determine which managers would be valuable assets to the new environment and which would not, who should be kept and who should be let go, who needed to be added, what systems needed to be adjusted, what was out of date, and what worked and what did not. Obtaining perspectives from others was vital to this process.

Whenever she enters a new organization (a new company or a new role within her current company), Sandy does not believe in "starting out with a large knife to do surgery on the organization." Whether she is in Singapore, New Jersey, or Spain, Sandy acknowledges the importance of taking time to read the organization.

Results of a survey by Catalyst and included in their report, "Women in U.S. Corporate Leadership: 2003," indicate that the top barriers impacting women's advancement to senior levels reflect "issues within the work environment, including exclusion from informal networks, gender-based stereotypes, and a lack of role models." Knowing what affects your environment's growth will help you determine why certain "plants" are growing, while others are not. The main elements to consider are the value system, leadership orientation, and organization style.

VALUE SYSTEM

Every organization has its own value system that is focused on the issues that the organization has identified as crucial to success. They are usually related to customers, sales, costs, innovation, and workforce. When employees support the organization's values, they can and do contribute to both the organization's and their individual achievement and success. If they do not support that value system, they will not be successful or feel a sense of fulfillment or job satisfaction. It is important that employees understand what the organization's value system is before they can support it.

When Betsy Wanner started her job search, an organization's value system was the most critical part of the environment that she assessed. It was important for her to stay attuned to how comfortable she felt with those she would work with and what they valued, and them with her. "I needed to be myself, and have that be okay," said Betsy. "Being excited about the possibilities was not enough. I needed them to be as excited about the possibility of working with me. I had eleven sessions with Disney people and in every case felt completely at home. The personality fit was unbelievable. We had so many things in common with regard to our approach to the work itself, interviews became more like discussions amongst colleagues on trials, tribulations, and opportunities in this type of work. After the interviews were over, we did not have the usual 'we know you can do this job' conversations. We talked about how much we liked each other and how excited we were to be working together—how thrilled we all were."

From 1984 through 1987, Beth Ziff, president of Customer Care Inc., worked for People Express airlines. The philosophy established a fertile environment in which employees thrived. Employees owned stock in the company, so they had an incentive to treat it with special care, as if it were their own. Everyone had specific teammates with whom they worked side by side. Having a partner/teammate offered them individuals who would cheer them on, whom they could vent to, and who would offer feedback. It allowed the building and sharing of trust. The company also believed there was always something new to be learned. Every week, employees sat together through a daylong training program on a variety of topics from team building to safety and industry updates. Twenty years later, the company's philosophy, which was practiced, not just preached, is something she pulls from in her career today.

In both Betsy's and Beth's cases, the organizations made visible commitments to a diverse workforce. When assessing the environment, it is particularly important to find out at what level of the organization these commitments are being made. Is the organization a traditional "topdown" leadership environment or is it a more "team-focused" organization? Is the organization one that is fast-paced, empowering leaders to act without major constraints—i.e., approval procedures, change in timelines, budgets, and so on—or is it an organization that moves slowly, with processes and procedures in place that cannot be circumvented? Does the organization foster open communication? Are all employees at every level involved in that process? Do they have access to information about their workplace and organizational plans? Can they add input to that process? Is the leadership one that is focused on employee development? Do the leaders provide appropriate ongoing support for employees during both good times and bad?

A colleague shared an example about the manager of a group of individuals who were experiencing a high degree of stress and lack of productivity due to a very large reduction of staffing in their organization and their area. The manager was barely visible during this entire distressing period and clearly did not recognize the need to make the commitment to spend time with his staff in order to help create a new and more positive workplace environment. Instead, he had the area refurbished and allowed the employees to select "the plant of their choice," which he believed would make them all feel better. As my colleague shared with me, the employees would have preferred to "burn the fern" and have the opportunity to talk with the manager instead. Clearly, this manager had no understanding of the importance of his role in helping the environment to grow and flourish. In the words of Walt Disney: "You can dream, create, design and build the most wonderful place in the world. . . but it requires people to make the dream a reality." Effective leaders know that environment is about more than location. Employees need an environment in which they feel valued. A corner office

> "EFFECTIVE LEADERS KNOW THAT ENVIRONMENT IS ABOUT MORE THAN LOCATION."

with windows is nice, but a sense of value and support goes a lot farther.

What Elements Can and Can't Be Changed?

Once you have assessed the elements, you must do a reality check on what can or cannot be changed in order to create a successful environment. For example, if in the assessment process there is an issue with flexible work hours, what can be done to address that issue?

In their report about one of their 2002 Award winners, Marriott International Inc., Catalyst reported that the organization "learned that flexibility in scheduling and attitudes toward long work hours are of primary importance to senior-level female leaders. . . . Marriott's commitment to work/life programs includes offering on-site, discounted child care, a free resource and referral line, an employee assistance program, and a family care spending account." Ernst & Young LLP, a 2003 Catalyst Award winner, is a "leader in creating flexible work arrangements for its people. For example, 2,000 professionals are using formal flexible arrangements of some kind—87 percent are women and 59 percent are partners, principals, or directors."

For leaders in the workplace, having that creative mind-set and the ability to implement these types of alternatives requires a flexible and adaptive orientation. If, for example, your workplace environment is a 24/7 operation and you or your employees are required to work on holidays, could you find a way to "outsource" or bring in temporary staff to make it possible for employees to have some holidays off? Could you create split shifts on those days that would allow employees to work only part of the day? Could you use an automated response system in lieu of staffing? Perhaps the issue of paid versus unpaid leave is an area that needs addressing.

In their summer 2003 edition, *Executive Female* magazine ran an article that reported: "94 percent of leave-takers who receive full pay return to their same employer. A smaller number of unpaid employees—76 percent—return. In addition, businesses with paid leave policies reduce absenteeism and healthcare costs while increasing productivity and enhancing recruitment efforts."

WHAT CAN'T BE CHANGED?

Leaders must also be realistic about their environment and what, perhaps, they cannot change. Attempting to change those things that are sacrosanct within an organization can, and oftentimes does, result not only in frustration but in negative results.

For example, we spoke above about flexible hours. However, they aren't realistic for every position within an organization. A colleague recently shared a story about a part-time employee who had been with a company for a number of years. The employee was responsible for billing, but as the company grew and the employee took more time off for her growing family, it was no longer an option to have her handle a time-sensitive responsibility. The billing function now required a full-time employee. The company attempted to accommodate her request for a flexible part-time position. However, the position was in another department, performing a job function that was of lesser responsibility but would certainly accommodate her needs as well as the needs of the company to replace her. The employee did not want to perform that job function and subsequently the company had to let her go.

As a leader, it is important to make every effort to listen to your employees' concerns and accommodate them if possible. However, you must be clear about what is required to perform the job function. If the employee is unwilling or unable to achieve, then he or she must understand that you will need to find a replacement who can. As much as we may want to be a supportive and caring leader, we do need to remember: "The business of business, is business!"

What Is Growing in Your Environment?

After identifying the type of environment in which you wish to work, assessing the elements affecting the environment, and what elements can and can't be changed, you need to identify what is growing within your environment. What is working and what is not? Like gardeners, leaders have to know what the existing "plants" are, why some thrive, and why others struggle.

Karen Nemetz Duvall said that because she has inherited so many teams, with such a variety of personalities and histories, she has been branded as a "fixer." Consequently, in a career spent in multiple industries and companies, she has joined companies with big problems and new CEOs. "They give me fat recruiting and severance budgets, assuming my first task will be a wholesale cleanup of the team. Time and time again, I am amazed at the resilience, commitment, talent, and drive of people who are freed from organizational dysfunction. The first few times I felt lucky to have found a star performer buried in the chaos. It did not take long to realize that stars instantly emerge in an environment of coaching, advocacy, and unencumbered passion."

"STARS INSTANTLY EMERGE IN AN ENVIRONMENT OF COACHING, ADVOCACY, AND UNENCUMBERED PASSION."

SUMMARY

Leaders must:

- CHOOSE AN ENVIRONMENT MOST CONDUCIVE TO THEIR GROWTH
- CONDUCT DUE DILIGENCE TO ASSESS THE ENVIRONMENT
- ASSESS THEIR VALUES AND NEEDS VERSUS THE ORGANIZATION'S VALUES AND NEEDS
- DETERMINE WHAT CAN AND CANNOT BE CHANGED
- ASSESS THEIR NEEDS FOR BALANCE VERSUS THE ORGANIZATION'S AND POSITION'S NEEDS AND REQUIREMENTS

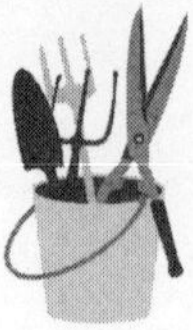

LEADERSHIP INVENTORY

1. Do you recognize and value the importance of the environment in fostering your leadership and career development?

What actions have you taken to identify the environment most conducive for you?

How has this contributed to your growth and development?

How has this contributed to your organization's success?

What resources/activities help you to choose and contribute to this environment?

When was the last time you used these resources/activities in pursuit of this goal?

2. Do you recognize and value the importance of conducting ongoing assessments of your environment?

What actions have you taken to assess your environment?

How has this contributed to your growth and development?

How has this contributed to your organization's success?

What resources/activities help you in pursuit of this goal?

When was the last time you used these resources in pursuit of this goal?

3. Do you recognize and value the importance of being flexible and adaptable in managing your environment and making any necessary modifications?

What actions have you taken to demonstrate this ability?

How has this contributed to your growth and development?

How has this contributed to your organization's success?

What resources/activities help you in pursuit of this goal?

When was the last time you used these resources/activities to achieve this goal?

Call to Action

Based upon your response to the Leadership Inventory, identify three (3) actions to further your continuing development and success as a leader.

Action	Timetable
1.	
2.	
3.	

CHAPTER FIVE

CREATING THE ENVIRONMENT

CHAPTER 5

CREATING THE ENVIRONMENT

> *"The great challenge for the garden designer is not to make the garden look natural, but to make the garden so that the people in it will feel natural."*
>
> *—Lawrence Halprin*

You have assessed your needs, evaluated the environment, and accepted what can and cannot be changed. You must now create the environment that fits your needs and vision. In gardening, ensuring you have the right environment—soil and moisture conditions, sun exposure, shade, and so on—for the plants you wish to grow is crucial to the eventual survival, growth, and maturation of those plants. Similarly, in the corporate world, the organizational or work environment is crucial to survival, growth, and maturation of individuals. When gardeners recognize that their environments are not conducive to certain plants or vice versa, they can attempt corrective action. Initially they might try to rectify such situations through direct intervention such as adding water and fertilizer. However, this is usually a short-term solution, if effective at all.

Eventually, the gardener must recognize that the plants need a different environment to grow and thrive. The same is true for developing people in the workplace. In the end, the leader must recognize there is no substitute for having the right environment as a starting point.

During a business trip that took me through Chicago's O'Hare Airport, I stopped to grab a bite to eat in one of the small concourse restaurants. My waitress was just delightful—efficient and pleasant. I noticed that all the employees were in such great spirits. Although the physical workspace was not particularly conducive to that behavior—rushed travelers, cramped spaces, awkward hours, noise—they all were helping each other and clearly enjoying their roles. I asked my waitress why she and the other staff seemed to enjoy what they did, and she said very quickly, "Oh, it's because of our manager. She is great!" She went on to explain how the manager made sure they had what they needed to do the job, was there to take care of problems if they needed her, and took care of issues in a manner considered firm but fair. The manager also made sure that she thanked the staff after every shift. If she was unable to be there, she would leave notes for people, especially if it was one of those awful snow-delay days for passengers.

No matter what the size or type of organization—be it a small airport eatery or a Fortune 500 company—the environment in which it is based determines the ultimate success of the organization. They need individuals who have the capabilities and the willingness to perform for them, and individuals need environments that are conducive to their growth and development. The O'Hare restaurant manager created an environment in which employees thrived and customers returned. She understood the importance of establishing a nurturing environment and treated employees as customers. Before I left the restaurant, I introduced myself to the manager and congratulated her on a job well done. Establishing an environment that helps employees blossom despite distracting elements around them is not easy to accomplish.

Leaders who establish environments that develop their employees know that by contributing to the individual's ongoing success, the leaders are also contributing to their own success. Anna Ball, CEO of Ball Seed Company, learned much of what she knows about business from her father. "A good leader," he told her, "has his roots down in the organization."

"A GOOD LEADER HAS HIS ROOTS DOWN IN THE ORGANIZATION."

"Having connections to all levels of employees is so critical for success," says Anna. "I started in our company working with line workers packeting seed. I have never lost that connection with the line workers. It gives you perspective and keeps you grounded." Today, Anna runs what she refers to as a "crunchy organization": "I try to avoid sogginess [a concept from the *Economist*, August 1987]. In crunchy organizations, actions have repercussions, goals are clear, cultures are apparent. Everyone knows what we stand for. This is not a state you arrive at and you're there. If you don't keep constantly fighting sogginess, you drift there very easily—especially as you grow in size." Part of fighting "sogginess" is continually assessing your organization and determining your immediate and future needs.

Determine Your Needs

As a leader with a desire to create an environment conducive to the development of others, you have done your homework and assessed the current environment and your role within that environment. What do you need to create your ideal environment? First, review the results of your assessment. What does your environment support? What is already growing? What is your role within the environment? What is the degree of flexibility within the environment for change? Are you starting from scratch and need to plant a brand-new garden? Or are you inheriting one that is already picture-perfect, requiring only ongoing maintenance? Is the garden one that may need only an updated, improved look? Or is it one that has been neglected, with a lot of the flowers and plants "gone to seed" and overrun with weeds?

> "What does your environment support?"

Following the events of September 11, 2001, Susan Sobbott and her employees had to move from their downtown New York offices. "We lost our offices, and had to find temporary space. Our corporate office staff was split among six locations in three different states because there was no place large enough to accommodate us." The new locations were a longer commute for some (over three hours) and also had failing phones, few computers, and limited office furniture. "We did a little bit of 'kitschy stuff' to get people comfortable, like 'welcome' signs and goodie bags. We spent the majority of our time talking to employees. We acknowledged the emotion of such dramatic change on the heels of traumatic events—and we had a business to run! We tried to create a support structure to help people adjust. We hired counselors to come in weekly. We gathered people together as much as we could. I used the leadership team as much as possible, tasking them with ensuring that their people were comfortable and the environment was the best we could possibly make it. For example, on a day's notice, I asked all of the vice presidents to come in and physically check the location of each expected employee and make sure that everything was in decent shape." After going into the new office space and assessing the situation, moving furniture and cleaning desks, Susan bought big tubs of cookies and candy, and water, wrote notes for every person's desk and did everything she could so that employees would have something that made them feel more comfortable—"more at home." In this situation, Susan was thrown from one environment into another, without time to make much of a plan. A good leader must learn how to improvise; however, in most circumstances, plans (even on short notice) are needed to ensure that the goals of the leader's envisioned environment are achieved.

DEVELOP A PLAN

As discussed in Chapter 2, in order to reach a destination, it is important to create the development plan to get you there. At Ball Seed Company, for example, the organization has identified "Four Pillars of Growth":

- **COLOR THE WORLD:** Be the number one supplier in every market worldwide.
- **CREATE EXCITEMENT IN THE WORLD OF FLOWERS:** Increase new products as a percent of sales, expand the product range in ornamentals, create three new "top 20" items in the next five years.
- **ALWAYS BE THE FIRST CHOICE FOR SERVICE:** Provide the best customer service in the industry at all times.
- **IMPROVE OUR COST POSITION:** Deliver optimum value through high-quality production and efficient operations.

In order to reach these pillars, Ball Seed Company has to continually evaluate each pillar, measure the results of the process established to obtain their goals, and evaluate the process for improvement. The same holds true for all organizations. In order to advance, organizations need plans that establish their goals and include tools for measurement and process improvement.

MEASUREMENT

What gets measured gets accomplished. When I served as a Malcolm Baldrige National Quality Award examiner, I found that many organizations had implemented processes that were designed to produce "estimated" results. In many instances, however, once the process was implemented there were very little measurements taken to determine the actual results—similar to those employees I mentioned in Chapter 3, who take self-assessment tests but put the results in a drawer, never pulling them out to use as measurements of growth. This tool should be used as you establish the environment to determine the results of the initial actions and serve as a "milestone" check as you move forward.

"WHAT GETS MEASURED GETS ACCOMPLISHED."

PROCESS IMPROVEMENT

This tool should be used once measurements are performed, if they indicate that results have fallen short of the desired goal. If, as an example, the initial staffing needs were underestimated or the workload exceeds original expectations, then the process improvement tool will determine what actions need to be taken to correct the problem. In the garden, for example, some plants will need a different fertilizer, while others may need to be relocated, pruned, or removed.

When I first assumed the responsibility for the customer service area at NCR, I reviewed the weekly customer inquiry reports and quickly determined that the headquarters-based customer service reps were spending 70 percent of their time responding to customer inquiries and complaints about minor dollar amounts. For example, customers often complained that their gas gauges indicated there was more gas in the tank than they were credited with having. Perhaps they said the tank was two-thirds full and they were charged for it being half full. The amount of each dispute was small—around $4. At that time, if a customer disputed any charge or had any type of complaint with the service, the frontline rental agents advised the customer to call or write to the customer service area at headquarters (and at that time there wasn't even a toll-free number). I immediately made a recommendation to give the frontline rental agents authority to make discretionary customer adjustments up to $25 without approval from headquarters. The result was a resounding success. I also established a toll-free number for those customers who still wanted to contact us for service. As a result, customer satisfaction levels improved dramatically. Employee satisfaction also improved dramatically, as frontline employees felt more empowered and were no longer faced with having to deal with unhappy customers. The workload of headquarters-based customer service representatives decreased and was reorganized, allowing many employees to take advantage of the

> "WITHOUT MEASURES FOR PROCESS IMPROVEMENT, THE STATUS QUO REMAINS THE SAME."

new flex hours and part-time opportunities. The cost savings for the organization were significant. By evaluating the current work procedures, I was able to measure the needs for adjustments and improvements. Without measures for process improvement, the status quo remains the same.

Plant Needs

People, like plants, have different qualities—all of which dictate the success of the garden. Once leaders assess and determine the types of environments they wish to create, they need to determine their staffing requirements. What qualities are needed? Perennials bloom year after year, while some plants bloom biannually, and annuals must be replanted each year. Some require the support of fences and trellises to grow, while others can stand on their own.

When determining staffing needs, it is important to consider diversity, experience, and style.

DIVERSITY

For ongoing success, it is vital that organizations recognize and value the need to select a wide variety of people. For example, in the spring, many gardeners fill their flower beds with plants such as pansies. They offer immediate color to gardens waiting for other plants and bulbs to awaken from their winter dormancy. Pansies are low maintenance and offer immediate satisfaction, yet you would be hard pressed to find a garden with nothing but pansies planted.

Diversity is a hallmark of organizations that value creativity and sustained growth. Michele Coleman Mayes calls diversity the spice of life. "I enjoy meeting people who are not like me and figuring out what is in the mix," said Michele. "When I assumed responsibility for supervising the international attorneys at Colgate, they numbered around 50. I had to get up to speed very quickly each time I was required to problem solve for a given country. That forced me to see the world from myriad perspectives."

"DIVERSITY IS A HALLMARK OF ORGANIZATIONS THAT VALUE CREATIVITY AND SUSTAINED GROWTH."

A variety of annuals and perennials is essential. Annuals serve well as part-time, temporary, or seasonal employees that are used for peak business periods or as experts and consultants for specific projects. Although they offer fresh dimensions, annuals have to be replanted season after season. Perennials, however, offer sustained growth, building upon the previous season's growth. For example, an executive participating in the WUI program "The Few" led the acquisition team of an organization that was acquiring another company. At a critical juncture of the merger, she had an accident resulting in hospitalization. Her perennials—those she had been mentoring and developing and who reported directly to her—were able to step in and manage the entire process with very little downtime and with minimal guidance from their leader.

Other aspects of having a garden filled with a myriad and diverse group of plants is that the tall plants can lend their support in providing shade for the smaller plants, and there are in fact several varieties of plants that actually need other plants to help them bloom.

The best teams I have led were those comprised of groups of individuals that brought an array of expertise and different styles. This diversity always results in the team members learning and growing, gaining broader business perspectives and developing mutual respect for one another's contributions.

The workplace has never been as diverse as it is today. That diversity has contributed to richness of thought and style, among other great attributes. It has also contributed to potential difficulties between older, middle-aged, and young employees. In all my years of working, there have always been issues between the older generation and the young "pups." I can remember being a twentysomething know-it-all employee looking at the forty-and-over employees, wondering how they were capable of getting out of bed and coming to work at their advanced age.

As I moved into that over-forty generation, I clearly remember looking at the twentysomethings entering the workplace and thinking I had underwear older than them. The generation-gap issue is an old one. However, the differences in the generations today are much more complex. If you look at the senior ranks of most corporations, many of the most senior managers are white males that the AARP is already calling "senior citizens."

Most of the workplace today is occupied by what we commonly refer to as the baby boomers. These individuals are currently in their forties and fifties. Add Generation X—those folks who today are in their thirties—and the Nexters—those young people graduating and entering the workplace for the first time. All of these individuals are valuable for what they can contribute and vital for the continued growth and prosperity of organizations. In considering the types of individuals for your environment, it is important to remember how very different these individuals are and how their needs will be different.

"A PROSPECTIVE LEADER MAY BE DETERMINED AND TENACIOUS, BUT IF HE DOES NOT UNDERSTAND THE CHARACTER OF HIS TIME, HE WILL FAIL."

Charles DeGaulle once said: "A prospective leader may be determined and tenacious, but if he does not understand the character of his time, he will fail." Leaders know that people are the "character" of the time. They understand the importance of attracting, retaining, and developing a diverse group of individuals.

EXPERIENCE AND SKILL LEVELS

What is experience? Experience is more than the number of years an individual has been on the job. As Aldous Huxley said: "Experience is not what happens to a man. It is what a man does with what happens to him."

In today's workforce, entry-level employees may have more experience with technology than senior management does. However, they do not usually possess the leadership skills found in employees that have managed and led teams of individuals for years. When deciding their staffing needs, leaders have to consider experience of potential employees in terms of skill, rather than simply age and number of years on the job.

Staffing decisions also need to be based upon the needs of the environment. Leaders have to determine the mix of experience levels. Do you have time for seeds to grow or do you need mature plants? When creating a new landscape, some may need entry-level "seedlings" to add a fresh perspective, while others may need more mature plants that are already capable of offering support to new growth and filling in bare spots.

If you have inherited a garden that simply requires a face-lift, you may simply require a mix of young and more mature plants. You may want to try a variety that you have not yet worked with. For example, multilingual and tech-savvy individuals may make a perfect fit even if they are right out of college. The skills outweigh the lack of years in the workplace.

Hiring entry-level employees may work for some projects, but for others, more experienced employees are needed. If you do not have time to grow plants from seeds, you may need to refresh or start a new garden with mature plants, relocating experienced employees from different jobs or departments.

STYLES AND ORIENTATIONS

Once you decide on the degree of diversity and experience of the plants you need, you have to explore styles and orientations. In his book *Peak Performers,* Charles Garfield describes three kinds of employees and likens them to animals. The first group are tigers. When I ask WUI participants about tigers and their behaviors, invariably the responses include: they are fast, aggressive, animals to be careful/wary of, and predators. Garfield's theory is that they are often those things, but those types of attributes inside a corporation really boil down to: They make things happen. They are the movers and the shakers and they get things done. Those kinds of people are essential in a corporation.

The next type of animal Garfield references is the elephant. When WUI groups share attributes of elephants, the answers include: they are slow, dependable, and loyal, have great memories, are methodical, and are reliable. Garfield says elephants watch things happen, noting how they occur to make sure that things go well. They look for the details, they collect the data, and they make sure that the ideas the tigers bring forth are implemented well. When I ask people to think about this type of individual in an organization—people who are dependable, reliable, methodical, and in my opinion the ones that have a great deal of information to share—participants agree we need these kind of people as well.

It is important to note that no one person is ever all tiger or all elephant. I am definitely a tiger 90 percent of the time. I like

"IT IS IMPORTANT TO NOTE THAT NO ONE PERSON IS EVER ALL TIGER OR ALL ELEPHANT."

to get things done and new ideas implemented quickly; however, my elephant side slows me down so I can process those great ideas. In addition, I make certain that I listen to the elephants on my teams who help me to see the pros and cons of my ideas. For example, Rosina Racioppi will often recommend that I "take a day" when I'm in my I-have-a-great-idea mode. She will often wait to see if I actually talk to her again about implementing that "great idea" or have determined it is not really what needs doing.

Michele Coleman Mayes, who is also without a doubt a tiger, will, when appropriate, make use of her elephant style. For example, she tells us, "I am not known for sugarcoating things. Yet, on numerous occasions, I have had to deliver what could be termed bad news. I am able to do this without alienating the listener. I have used this skill in so many settings. For example, in negotiating with opposing counsel, discharging employees for poor performance, and advising senior management. I think I draw on a number of attributes to do this: listening, communicating, a sense of humor, and empathizing."

I subscribe to the theory that tigers and elephants working as a team are awesome. It is also important to recognize that either one of these types of individuals can be and are in many instances very successful leaders.

The third group of workplace "animals" Garfield describes are hippos. Whenever I mention hippos to groups I am working with, there is often a great deal of laughter. The groups invariably describe hippos in the workplace as miserable, wallowing in the mud, big and unmovable, averse to change; they like to drag other people into the hippo pool with them; they are negative people.

> "TIGERS AND ELEPHANTS WORKING AS A TEAM ARE AWESOME."

Just as most individuals are a mix of tigers and elephants, most also have a bit of hippo in them. When I am in a blue mood, the tiger in me motivates the hippo to get moving, and the elephant helps me refocus. Some people become so bogged down that they need outside help from tigers and elephants.

When I ask groups what they think might be the number of hippos in the workplace, I hear estimates that 50 percent to 90 percent of employees occupy the spot called "hippodum." If hippos have such negative qualities, why are there so many in the workplace? Hippos often enter organizations with tiger and elephant instincts. They often become hippos through lack of attention and neglect, and they simply give up on being contributors. In Chapter 8, I will discuss how to motivate potential hippos.

So, when you are considering the types of employees for your organization, you need to consider the possibility that some might turn into hippos. For example, in the garden there are a number of types of vines. They usually grow quickly, and are beautiful and hardy despite their delicate size. Unfortunately, when neglected, they can take over other sections of your garden, pulling other plants down and often strangling the possibility for growth. For this reason, such "hippo vines" must be cared for and given attention. Vines such as morning glories may seem ordinary, their contribution to the garden unnoticed by the inexperienced or unobservant. Such a vine can easily be ignored. Once it "goes to seed," though, it can make a horrendous mess and can become difficult to remove.

Pick Your Plants

Seed packets are the résumés of plants. They let gardeners know if the seeds have the credentials to be successful within the gardeners' environments. They offer pictures of the plants the seeds will grow in to, and advice on the environment best suited for the plants and how to grow them. In selecting people, leaders look for similar information. Leaders review the potential employees' skills and credentials in the form of résumés and recommendations to assess their qualifications, styles, and motivations.

Be wary of planting unlabeled plants. For example, when Jack Yurish was an executive vice president and owner of NCR, a former colleague and close friend, who was suffering from a terminal illness, called and asked if Jack could find employment for his eldest son, a recent college graduate. Athough the graduate was an "unlabeled plant"—meaning Jack knew little about the graduate's work experience and ethics—Jack indicated that his company was establishing a new management development program for supervisory level managers, and he could hire his colleague's son as a participant in that program sight unseen.

The program was a "study-work-study" approach spread over several months, with classroom work being interspersed with on-job performance. During the course of the program, it became evident that while the young graduate was extremely bright, he was not interested in the car rental industry. Not only was he bored with the type of work offered, but his disruptive style—predominantly use of wit and sarcasm—caused other employees discomfort.

At the end of the program, a decision was made to sever him from the company, rather than promote him into a supervisory position with the other participants. The young man was intelligent, articulate, and well-read. It seemed to Jack, and others, that his abilities were more suited to writing, publishing, or teaching. Operating from that rationale, Jack first contacted his father to inform him of the decision. Initially the father was disappointed. However, after hearing Jack's assessment of his son's abilities and potential, he agreed with the assessment. Jack also assured him that the organization would be taking steps to help his son bridge to another career.

Next, Jack had a similar conversation with the son. He informed him of the decision, then discussed several career possibilities for the future and the help he and the company were prepared to give him to bridge to the future. Over the next several weeks, with the assistance provided by the organization's outplacement service, its human resource group, and personal contacts, the young man secured a job in publishing, an industry in which he went on to thrive—once again affirming that, just as plants in a garden, human beings need the right environment in order for them to flourish, grow, and be successful.

I also avoid sparse-looking plants. Entry-level individuals are the exception, as they understandably will not have a lot on their résumés. However, warning flags go up when I read the résumés of individuals who have not been in the workforce for many years and have made frequent moves. These individuals may have some of the required experience, but may need more serious grooming and handholding than the organization can provide at a given time.

The job history and skill sets highlighted on résumés share a lot of insight. For those I do interview, I am interested in knowing why he or she left the previous position and what his or her three greatest achievements are. From their answers, I obtain a sense of individuality. For example, some have told me about individuals they have managed and developed who have gone on to greater opportunities as a result of working in the potential employee's area. Individuals often share the process improvements they have made—cost savings, higher productivity, better services or products for an end user, and so on.

I also ask employees for the least satisfying areas of the job functions they have performed. In the past, I've been told that it was not satisfying to work in an environment in which the employee was expected to be a follower—where the expectation was for straight implementation of others' ideas, without room for creativity. Such individuals express upset over following the orders of others rather than being able to be innovative and contribute more.

I also ask about the three skills they feel they could bring to the job and the areas in which they know they need to improve. For example, I always ask about operating style. How do they prefer to get information? Orally, or written instruction? Do they learn better by studying or doing, or a combination of both? How do they feel about being the new kid on the block, especially if they were at the top of the team in their previous position? How will they feel about being teamed up with people they feel may not have the knowledge base they have?

I also look to see if the individual has taken the initiative to continue to develop himself or herself. Have they gone back to school and taken courses to improve in specific areas such as financial understanding or communication skills?

No matter what a person tells you in an interview, what their skill level appears to be, and what you may have heard from others with whom they have worked, it is a "guttuitiveness" about the person that helps to determine whether they are selected. At the end of the day, there is still a risk with everyone you hire.

> "IT IS A 'GUTTUITIVENESS' ABOUT THE PERSON THAT HELPS TO DETERMINE WHETHER THEY ARE SELECTED."

Once you have completed the assessment of the area and determined your plan, your task will be much easier if you have a network to assist you. It will help to gain the support and advice from others within the organization and externally who can assist you in your desire to create a successful environment. This may include other managers in the organization that can identify and recommend high performers who could contribute to your area—such as the human resources representative who understands your vision, and external colleagues who could recommend suitable candidates.

Setting the Basic Structure

Once a person is selected for a position, the leader's task is not complete. It has just begun. Gardeners must commit to continuously evaluating the soil and other conditions to determine what plants need assistance in the growth process. The same is true of leaders. Constant adjusting and adapting to changing conditions is necessary to maintain peak performance for individuals and continued growth for organizations.

After determining what is needed in their areas, successful leaders know each individual has different needs and requires individual support systems to thrive. Sadly, I often hear from women in our programs that they have little or no contact with their manager unless there is a crisis or until their yearly review. If they are brand-new "seedlings" they will need a great deal of attention in the early stages of their growth and as they adjust to their new environment. Without this initial attention, they may not become the wonderful flowers shown on their seed packets. Initially, these seedlings may need more care than you can give. It may be wise to obtain help from others. Senior employees would be outstanding mentors and support systems. They would benefit from assisting new employees by having the opportunity to develop their leadership skills. If you plan to relocate some plants, there will be a need to give them extra attention as they go through "transplant shock." They will need time to adjust to the new environment and may at first wilt and be very unattractive, but time and support will serve to allow these plants to spring back and bloom even better than before, in many instances.

"CONSTANT ADJUSTING AND ADAPTING TO CHANGING CONDITIONS IS NECESSARY TO MAINTAIN PEAK PERFOMANCE FOR INDIVIDUALS AND CONTINUED GROWTH FOR ORGANIZATIONS."

And, of course, when you plant a new garden, especially with fresh new seedlings, you still have to keep a careful watch for exposure to too much sunlight, overwatering and overfertilizing, and predators that will eat the plants. In the workplace, you may need to "shoo away" those who are not willing to give the entry-level or relocated employees a chance. Expose the new employees gradually to their new environment. Give them a chance to root and be sturdy before they have to face stressful conditions.

As I began to assume new responsibilities in my career at NCR, and as I built the WUI organization, I needed to continuously focus on what I, as the leader, had to do to help foster a productive workplace environment that would result in the growth and success of both the organization and the people. At NCR, prior to the new ownership, I had been responsible for the customer service and sales training area. I had several perennial managers reporting to me as well as their large group of employees, all of whom were very comfortable with our respective roles, styles, and mutual expectations. We had a long-term track record of identifying areas needing to be addressed and we knew who had the responsibility for addressing each type of issue. As I took on other areas of responsibility within the company, I inherited a new group of perennial managers and their employees. During the transition, many of those managers assimilated very well into the changing environment, but some did not.

During this transition period, there were many issues that required careful consideration and needed to be addressed. The new seeds and plants, and the transplanted perennials that had no experience with my leadership experience or abilities, nor with each other, needed the opportunity and time to express their needs, concerns, etc., with me. I too needed that opportunity to share my vision and expectations. In addition, I had to pay very close attention to the perennials who were concerned that I would not be able to give them the attention to which they had become accustomed.

My first action was to meet with my old gang, my existing group, and ask for their help and understanding. I explained that I was going to rely heavily on them in this transition period and I needed them to operate without my involvement during this period, unless it was of critical importance. Then I held a department head meeting involving all of the managers, both old and new. I also brought in managers who, though not located at headquarters, also reported to me. This gave everyone the opportunity to hear my vision and expectations and to listen to each other's. I made sure there was an opportunity for them to meet with all the senior executives in the company, and I built in time for personal interaction where each really had the opportunity to get to know one another more personally. At that time, I also had all of the managers participate in a Styles Assessment Workshop, which helped them all understand their strengths and how they each contributed to the team. When all of the managers participated in the Styles Assessment, I shared with them my Style Profile.

Next, I met individually with each of the managers who would be reporting to me, to set up regularly scheduled meetings with them to identify any mutual areas of concern and discuss our mutual expectations and operating styles as identified by the assessment.

The next step was to conduct an all-employee meeting in which I was able to communicate the organization's vision and the mutually agreed action that all of the managers and I had established. I asked for their support, recommendations, and concerns. I stressed we were no longer in individual silos but one team working toward making NCR what we all dreamed it would be. We agreed to hold these meetings quarterly and we sent a weekly update to all the employees, sharing our success stories and other noteworthy news. Every day, whenever my schedule permitted, I conducted five-minute stand-up meetings at the beginning or the end of the day with all my management team, simply to touch base, keep them informed, and find out what was going on with them. It was also very important to keep the regional managers, those who were not in the corporate headquarters, in the loop. In addition to a weekly conference call, they were required to attend monthly meetings at headquarters. I encouraged my management team to take every opportunity to spend time getting to understand each other's area of expertise. This contributed to a far more knowledgeable and productive team and to their developing their own individual learning and growth. This process allowed me to establish an early warning detection system, or tool, if you will, rather like an outside barometer or rain gauge in the garden. I could very easily and quickly identify issues and take the necessary actions to address them. It also allowed me to spot weeds or other potential dangers in the environment.

In the final selection process, a successful leader can usually tell whether or not the candidate will be a fit for their new environment. Asking what the candidate values in the workplace, and what they most liked and disliked in their previous jobs, enables the leader to assess that candidate's possibility for success. Speaking with previous employers and personal references, if possible, can provide additional information about a potential employee. Even better, having the candidate meet with existing team members and getting their perspective can help the leader determine if this person will be a fit.

FERTILIZERS

Fertilizing is an essential part of setting the basic structure. There is certainly no shortage of fertilizers and plant foods in most workplaces—so many workplaces have an overabundance of "experts" who are only too happy to share their knowledge and recommendations (even if not asked to do so). Unfortunately, as with plants in the garden, there is no one-strength-fits-all fertilizer for employees in the workplace.

> "FERTILIZATION IS AN ESSENTIAL PART OF SETTING THE BASIC STRUCTURE."

In the office, aside from the advice of others, fertilizers might be workshops, office-sponsored memberships to professional associations, networking events, and magazine and newspaper subscriptions to trade publications.

Occasionally, even with the best interest of the employee at heart, leaders make the wrong fertilizing decision. In the garden, there are a number of lawns that have suffered the "burnt" look of overfertilization. Such gardeners didn't pay attention to the lawns' needs, instead acting upon what they thought the lawns might need. In business, listening to what the employees tell you they need in addition to what you believe is appropriate for them, rather than simply dumping the plant food that is available, is far more productive and cost effective—and appreciated by the employees. Years ago I was required to attend a session on the appropriate use of overheads, when my job function at the time was as head of organizational development for the company. I had 20 years of presentation experience—it was simply a waste of time and money and did nothing for my growth and development.

For their own growth, I encourage women to make the time to stay up-to-date on current events. In addition to business news, we need to know what is going on outside of our business and our industry. What is going on in our community? What is going on in our world? Making the time each day to gain some knowledge that is outside of our small world is valuable in social and business interactions—in addition to personal development.

SUMMARY

Gloria Steinem said: "Nature doesn't move in a straight line, and as part of nature, neither do we." Leaders must remember that while they are actively redeveloping or creating an environment, the environment is actively making changes of its own. The gardener cannot control elements such as rain and snow. In business, the leader must remember to focus on the possibilities. What unexpected flower will sprout as a result of a bird dropping a seed? What plants will suffer from unwanted slugs? The environment is always changing and the leader must work to keep up with the changes, while implementing changes of his or her own. Creating and developing an environment includes:

"NATURE DOESN'T MOVE IN A STRAIGHT LINE, AND AS PART OF NATURE, NEITHER DO WE."

- Determining your needs
- Developing a plan
- Implementing tools for measurement and process improvement
- Evaluating the pros and cons of diversity; experience and skill levels; and styles and orientations
- Selecting a variety of seeds and plants
- Setting the basic structure
- Fertilizers

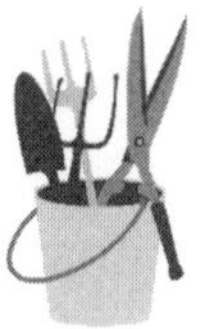

LEADERSHIP INVENTORY

1. Do you recognize and value the importance of creating an environment that fosters the development of others?

What actions have you taken to create this environment?

How has this contributed to your growth and development?

How has this contributed to the growth and development of others?

How has this contributed to your organization's success?

What resources/activities help you in pursuit of this goal?

When was the last time you used these resources/activities in pursuit of this goal?

2. Do you recognize and value the importance of identifying and selecting employees with diverse backgrounds, experiences, skills, and styles?

What actions have you taken to achieve this goal?

How has this contributed to your growth and development?

How has this contributed to the growth and development of others?

How has this contributed to your organization's success?

What resources/activities help you in pursuit of this goal?

When was the last time you used these resources/activities in pursuit of this goal?

3. Do you recognize and value the importance of continuously assessing both the environmental and individual needs?

What actions have you taken to achieve this goal?

How has this contributed to your growth and development?

How has this contributed to the growth and development of others?

How has this contributed to your organization's success?

What resources/activities help you in pursuit of this goal?

When was the last time you used these resources/activities to achieve this goal?

CALL TO ACTION

Based upon your response to the Leadership Inventory, identify three (3) actions to further your continuing development and success as a leader.

Action	Timetable
1.	
2.	
3.	

CHAPTER SIX

SUPPORTING THE ENVIRONMENT

CHAPTER 6

SUPPORTING THE ENVIRONMENT

> *"A leader does not learn and grow in isolation."*
>
> *—Lois Borland Hart*

Hollyhocks. Peonies. Dahlias. These are the stars of many gardens, yet without support systems to prop them up, they fall to the ground and fail to achieve their potential. In corporate America, many potential "stars" are also heads-down, sitting in their cubicles, working at their jobs very diligently, doing what is required, never exercising their full capabilities. Their talents are seldom known by individuals other than their own managers. And, sometimes, their own managers do not know just how much talent these people have. This is one reason why I was compelled to create WUI. The development of strategic alliances is an area that so many women need to more fully appreciate, understand, and take the opportunity to create for themselves so that they will be appreciated and rewarded for their efforts.

No matter what you call them—managers, mentors, champions, coaches, business colleagues, networks—individuals who offer support are strategic alliances. In this day and age of reorganization and restructuring, it is vital for professionals at all levels—from CEOs to secretaries—to develop strategic alliances for themselves and to help others create alliances for themselves.

I look back with tremendous appreciation for the people in my life: family, teachers, managers, and friends who helped support and coach me through the years. Today my strongest strategic alliances are my WUI network, Jack Yurish, and my sister, Susan Bush, who help me to see that my ideas are worthy of pursuing. They give me that "atta girl" when I need an "atta girl." In the garden, they would be trellises or stakes. Although I have done the growing, they continuously offer me the support needed to flourish. We need such people in our lives—those that can act as a sounding board, a cheerleader, a coach, an ear, all those things that make it possible for us to be much more successful.

"WE NEED SUCH PEOPLE IN OUR LIVES—THOSE THAT CAN ACT AS A SOUNDING BOARD, A CHEERLEADER, A COACH, AN EAR, ALL THOSE THINGS THAT MAKE IT POSSIBLE FOR US TO BE MUCH MORE SUCCESSFUL."

Who were the people in your life who offered a different view, or sound advice, or were there to offer help to you when you were feeling uncomfortable or afraid? For Michele Coleman Mayes, "Some were bosses, some were mentors, and others were just good friends. I'd say my mom had the greatest impact on me. She is one determined person. When she sets her mind to do something, nothing, and I mean nothing, gets in her way."

Many times we look back and think of parents, grandparents, an aunt, an uncle, somebody who truly valued our lives and helped "clear the cobwebs" and give us the sense of "I can do it, I'm very capable, I can do this thing." When you started school, some of you had teachers, coaches, friends, that were always there to be supportive, always there to help you think through a problem. In my own case, ever since I was a small child, I had people that I was able to turn to who were able to help me recognize things in myself that I did not always see.

My father was my earliest mentor. He always encouraged me and told me I was capable of doing anything I put my mind to. In high school, one of my role models was a woman by the name of Mrs. Noonan. She was a math and science teacher. Instead of constantly criticizing, she encouraged. If a student did not get something right, if she needed to make better grades, Mrs. Noonan would sit with the student and ask what could be done better. She always gave me the feeling that I was capable, but that I might just need a little more help or time to "make the grade." Today I reflect on her as a role model for teaching how to get the best out of people. Rather than being discouraging and only pointing out what is wrong, it is more helpful to show individuals what they have within themselves.

When Debbie Murphy joined IBM in 1973 as a secretary, she had a two-year degree in secretarial science and believed that would be her profession within IBM. When she became an executive secretary to IBM's chairman of the board in 1980, and then an administrative manager within the chairman's office, she realized she had the potential to do much more at IBM. Debbie went back to college on weekends to obtain a bachelor of science degree. In 1983 she made a significant career change from administration into information technology. This choice led to her first executive position in 1995 as a director, and subsequently to vice president in 1998. "I was very much helped along the way by several managers and executives who reached out to guide me, mentor me, and support me to take risks and advance confidently because I knew they were behind me all the way," said Debbie. "I did not achieve my success within IBM without the support and guidance of many people. It has been my absolute pleasure to give back to others along the way to help them achieve career success."

PAYING IT FORWARD

You cannot light another's path without brightening your own" is one of my favorite sayings. Just as it is important for leaders to create a shared vision with their employees and colleagues, it is equally important to help create and be strategic alliances with and for them. Such alliances promote growth for the employees and organization, and ultimately for the leader.

> "You cannot light another's path without brightening your own."

Over 80 percent of the men and women who have served as mentors in the WUI programs nationwide continue to participate every year, as new groups of women enroll in the WUI leadership development programs. They do not just volunteer their time and expertise because they enjoy helping others or because they want to give something back. It is because they, too, continue to learn and grow from the experience. For example, many of today's up-and-coming leaders are more technologically versed than the executives they are following. The young leaders benefit from the executives' years of experience, while the executives benefit from the young leaders' perspectives and different skill sets. Debra Hollinrake, WUI's administrative manager and technology whiz kid, is my tech mentor. Today's technology has grown and changed quickly. Many of today's senior business leaders reached their positions when this technology did not exist and now require mentoring from the younger "tech set."

Years ago I had an employee whose former boss was one of the original examiners for the Malcolm Baldrige National Quality Award. When I applied to become an examiner, the application process required business and personal references. My employee reached out to his previous boss, a senior Baldrige examiner, and introduced me to him. The former boss, in turn, recommended me and even helped me prep for the test to become an examiner.

A DIFFERENT VIEW

Strategic alliances offer a number of benefits. One of the first is a different view. Many of us have been in the position of trying to figure out a complex problem. This process is always easier when there is someone else in our network who we can turn to and ask how they might approach the problem. Jim Abrams once said: "A smart businessperson is one who makes a mistake, learns from it, and never makes it again. A wise businessperson is one who finds a smart businessperson and learns from him how to avoid the mistakes he made." Gaining that different perspective can save so much time and energy and, in fact, be so much more valuable than just having one thought or opinion on how to accomplish something.

At WUI, we practice a "Yes, and" philosophy. I started this while at NCR. When my team would look at how to improve a process or create a new service, everyone was asked to share one idea in turn. No one was allowed to interrupt or say anything negative. Everyone, however, was encouraged to add to the idea or make a suggestion that might be a little different by saying: "Yes, and how about this. . . ." This group alliance sets the tone for the meeting, opening up the floor to diverse thoughts and ideas. It was wonderful to witness that kind of creativity and expertise within the group.

MULTILEVEL SUPPORT

Strategic alliances or mentors in the olden days, if you will, were experienced executives who took on "apprentices" and molded them into their likenesses—the days of "if you do these things you too can be like me." In today's world, and particularly from the WUI perspective, we can and should form strategic alliances at many different levels within and outside an organization. Over the past 11 years, Michele Coleman Mayes has had positions that necessitated her leading people who knew a great deal more than she did in specific areas. "I understood that going in and worked hard to harness their knowledge," said Michele. "I needed for them to teach me, but at the same time accept me as their leader." For this reason, one of Michele's pieces of advice to women entering corporate America is: "Keep both hands outstretched—one to look for your mentors and the other to extend to others in need. And remember mentors should be as varied as the problems and issues being confronted."

As Michele continuously experienced, strategic alliances are about more than having the support necessary from senior level management. The savvy person knows the value of not being viewed as someone who only wants to mingle with people they think can get them somewhere, people they can benefit from knowing. A savvy person is someone who recognizes how everybody in the corporation has value and is a potential ally. Some of the greatest allies in corporations are the administrative assistants. Too often they are neglected by people who think they are lower-level employees that they do not need to affiliate themselves with. Nothing could be more incorrect.

As I was rising in business, many of my opportunities to interact with senior executives were the results of the relationships I had built with the administrative assistants. Because I had built such close relationships, they wanted me to succeed. It was amazing how much time I managed to have with senior staff because the administrative people put me on the calendar.

It is also important for leaders to develop alliances among peers, and encourage the people who directly report to them to do the same. Your peers have experiences and knowledge you can tap. They may have already been through something they could share with you to help you. They certainly have a network that would be highly valuable for you to be connected to. One world-renowned organization with which WUI partners moved its headquarters from New Jersey to California, where many of the key employees were offered positions. For various reasons, some employees were unable to make the move. Two such employees reached out to their mentors and peers in WUI. Within three weeks, they were offered positions at other New Jersey-based corporations. This all occurred because these individuals had an established network and recognized the importance of being able to ask for help.

> "IT IS ALSO IMPORTANT FOR LEADERS TO DEVELOP ALLIANCES AMONG PEERS, AND ENCOURAGE THE PEOPLE WHO DIRECTLY REPORT TO THEM TO DO THE SAME."

In 2000, when IBM was a Catalyst Award winner, it was cited as an organization that encourages employees to seek out mentors on their own. Former CEO Lou Gerstner personally discussed the development plans and leadership strengths of each individual brought forward by members of the Corporate Executive Committee. All employees were assigned at least one mentor on their Individual Development Plans, and were encouraged to seek out more mentors on their own.

One important reason to encourage employees to seek mentors on their own is that it will offer them a network of checks and balances—colleagues who will offer validation or let them know if they need to shift their behaviors or thoughts on a certain subject.

Developing Strategic Alliances

If you went to work tomorrow and found you were being restructured out of your position and perhaps out of your company, who would you reach out to? Who knows your capabilities? Who has personal awareness of your accomplishments? With whom have you networked and created the kind of alliance that allows you easily to pick up the phone and ask for help?

How do you go about developing alliances? How do you develop them for yourself and for others? This goes back to a very simple premise that I believe you will see throughout this book. It is my firm belief that we all have to ask for what we need. For leaders helping others develop strategic alliances, it is also about recognizing potential leaders and being their first supports.

When Jeffrey Hendrickson, now chief operating officer of Velocity Express, worked with Jack Yurish at NCR, he noted how Jack was always searching for individuals' strengths. "I can remember a time when Jack recommended transferring a struggling attorney in the law department to a sales department support role," said Jeffrey. "Ultimately, that individual wound up running a very successful direct sales operation. No one but Jack could see the potential for this individual and that sales agreement negotiation would become his 'power alley.'"

Individuals also have to demonstrate that they are willing to work. It's amazing how many people would get so much more from life if they simply asked for what it is they really wanted. What is the worse possible thing that can happen? Nothing other than that this may not be the right person to ask or the right time to ask for it. Perhaps we need to ask another person or the same person at a different time. If you are in a company where there is a mentor program, sign up or encourage your employees to sign up for the program. If there is not a structured one, or even if there is a structured process, create your own alliances at all different levels within the organization and be the beneficiary of those relationships.

If you are uncomfortable asking someone to be a mentor or an alliance, consider taking the step as another way to grow yourself. We always learn when we step outside our comfort zone. As Peter Drucker once said: "Whenever you see a successful business, someone made a courageous decision." The same holds true for the individual. Personal success is a series of hard decisions. Having someone to consult will make the decision-making process easier and help you make the most advantageous choices.

> "WE ALWAYS LEARN WHEN WE STEP OUTSIDE OUR COMFORT ZONE."

Whether you are looking for an alliance or you are establishing an alliance for others, the first place to start is with the manager. Ask what ideas/thoughts he or she may have on how to build alliances with others. Your manager is the first person you want as an alliance. Once you are comfortable speaking with him or her, move on to speaking with others, working on your level of comfort—even if it is a question of starting very small and making a point to talk to others at your own level before moving up the ladder.

Denise Yohn, vice president of segment marketing and brand planning for Sony Electronics Incorporated, began reaching out to people who she believed would yield considerable influence in her organization's future. "I sought out ways to demonstrate my and my group's expertise to these people and to partner with them on any initiative of mutual benefit," said Denise. One of these individuals was named to head a new department and Denise was asked to be a part of his group. "Not only has the relationship I had proactively developed with this person provided a great new opportunity in my career, it will also make it much easier for me to work with him in this new opportunity because the foundation of credibility and mutual trust already exists."

One of the smartest things you can do in creating strategic alliances is to go to people outside of your own area. If you want to learn more about other divisions in the company, go to the people running those areas and tell them you are interested in knowing more about their process, what they do, how they do it, how it fits into the corporate objectives. I have found people to be forthcoming and helpful when they have been asked in this way. When you go to people to ask for their opinions, their backgrounds, how they accomplished things, it also gives you a tremendous opportunity to showcase your talent. Because as they tell you about themselves, you have an opportunity to talk about yourself, your desires, your objectives, your skill base, which gives them an opportunity to know you more.

When we discuss these types of ideas in the WUI programs, I'm sometimes asked, Is it threatening to go outside a department to talk to other people? Will managers feel that they should be their employees' only source of advice? Will they feel threatened? The answer, very simply, is no. A manager will not argue with his or her employees if they tell the manager that what they are doing will help to make them better employees by gaining perspective about how the company operates. It would be very difficult for a manager to disagree.

For many individuals, the best place to practice building strategic alliances is outside the workplace. Most individuals have the opportunity to network and practice making alliances through their professional associations and organizations, places of worship, school districts if they have children, organizations such as the YWCA, or at their gym—all of these places give you the opportunity to meet and ask others for advice.

IT'S NOT WHAT YOU KNOW, IT'S WHO KNOWS YOU KNOW

Successful mentor/mentee relationships are based on both sides having goals and demonstrating they are willing to work for what they want. Demonstrate to potential mentors that you are willing to work if given the help. When I ask women in the workshops how they feel about demonstrating their competence, oftentimes I'll hear that they view it as bragging, or showing off, or not really necessary—"My work speaks for itself." In some cases that may be true, but in most cases, the person who gets the opportunity to demonstrate their competence has a better chance of being successful, being viewed as a success, and developing alliances, than the person who believes that they don't have to show what they do, or talk about what they do.

Susan Kendrick now runs the Southern Region for WUI. Years ago, she was a training manager for NCR's Orlando location. In that role, she implemented and ran training programs that were created by others at corporate headquarters. She was not responsible for the creation of the programs. She took advantage of an opportunity that presented itself when NCR implemented the Quality Improvement Process. She volunteered to be one of the quality improvement process trainers as NCR embarked on a nationwide program to train thousands of employees across the country from entry level to the most senior executives.

Susan and I attended the same training session at Quality College, where I had the opportunity to observe Susan when she made a presentation that she had created. The topic was a very basic, mundane one and was not anything very exciting. However, Susan created another approach and facilitated the discussion in such a way that everyone was truly impressed by her creativity. She engaged everyone in the process and made it a highly interactive and energizing workshop. What she created became something that was used across the country. By taking that opportunity to demonstrate her competence by showcasing her creative talent, she was very shortly thereafter promoted to regional training director, responsible for creating and implementing new programs nationwide.

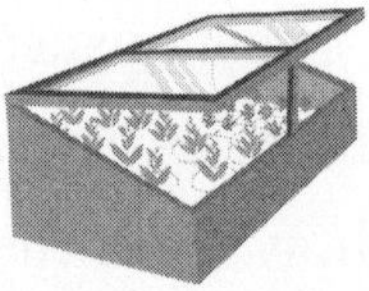

CRUCIAL ASSOCIATES

In the organizational savvy workshops we conduct for WUI and other organizations, we advise the groups that one of the most important aspects of being a savvy individual has to do with being a crucial associate. Simply put, it is being the eyes and ears of your manager—someone who is regarded by the manager as the go-to person. Your manager is one of your most important strategic alliances. The crucial associate will always help the manager know what is happening, what is working well, and what isn't.

If the manager has implemented a new process and asks an employee how well the process is working, the manager expects an honest reply. A crucial associate who knows that there are problems needs to say, "I know that this new process is designed to do X, but there are some modifications that need to be made so we can achieve that result. I've investigated it and I've gotten some input from the people who are actually implementing the process. Here are three things we can do very simply to enhance the process so it will achieve the results you had envisioned." What has the employee done? He or she has given the manager the opportunity to make the process work well. Your responsibility to your manager is to work well with him or her so that the results that all of you want are achieved. Do not work against the manager and hold back information he or she can act on, and above all, go to the manager not with problems but with answers. The person who can help the manager make decisions and succeed is the person who is going to be considered a crucial associate. When I look back at my own career, both as reporting to a manager or having people reporting to me, there is no question that that one aspect is something that definitely made a difference in my career. Employees who came to me to identify problems, propose solutions, and request my help and support always received my respect and gratitude. They were the people who

> "ONE OF THE MOST IMPORTANT ASPECTS OF BEING A SAVVY INDIVIDUAL HAS TO DO WITH BEING A CRUCIAL ASSOCIATE."

were promoted. Honesty, courage, and credibility are attributes I respect.

One of the other dilemmas we have a great deal of discussion about is the question of whether or not it is ever appropriate to go over your manager's head or around your manager. Unless the issue is a serious matter, such as ethics or sexual harassment, which should clearly be discussed with the human resources department, it is always in the employees' best interest to talk with the manager. Never go over your manager's head or talk with others about your manager's decisions without first talking with your manager. If you feel your manager is unresponsive, get help from your strategic alliances who might be able to talk with your manager with you. If you feel it necessary to talk with your manager's manager, tell your manager what you are doing. Remember, support works both ways. Ask your manager to be part of the meeting, but never make the mistake of talking negatively about your manager to other people, or going around or above your manager without good cause.

ARE YOU MAKING A DIFFERENCE?

In the WUI programs, I ask the participants if they can easily and quickly identify the last five:

- Nobel Peace Prize winners

- Heismann Trophy winners
- Miss America winners

I've never had a group that could identify all five in any of these categories. However, whenever I ask them to identify the five people in their lives that have made a significant difference, those people are quickly and easily identified.

The point is that all of those who made headline news at the time were not remembered, but the people who made a difference in the participants lives were. I urge all the WUI graduates to make a commitment that they too will be remembered on others' personal lists of five. Ralph Waldo Emerson said: "It is one of the most beautiful compensations of this life that no man can sincerely try to help another without helping himself."

"IT IS ONE OF THE MOST BEAUTIFUL COMPENSATIONS OF THIS LIFE THAT NO MAN CAN SINCERELY TRY TO HELP ANOTHER WITHOUT HELPING HIMSELF."

SUMMARY

Everyone needs someone in their life who will help them achieve their potential. Serena and Venus Williams, Michelle Qwan, Mia Hamm, and Tiger Woods all have coaches who point out their areas for improvement and encourage them. No matter what level leaders and employees reach, strategic alliances are still vital.

Developing strategic alliances is a win-win all the way around. Leaders and their employees must:

- Develop multilevel support
- Become crucial associates
- Pay it forward
- Enjoy the view

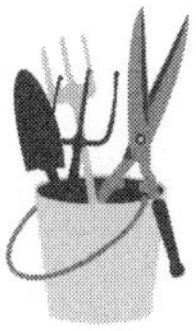

LEADERSHIP INVENTORY

1. Do you recognize and value the importance of creating and maintaining internal and external strategic alliances?

What actions have you taken to create and maintain those alliances?

How has this contributed to your growth and development?

How has this contributed to your organization's success?

What resources/activities help you create those alliances?

When was the last time you used these resources/activities in pursuit of this goal?

2. Do you recognize and value the importance of helping others to create internal and external strategic alliances?

What actions have you taken to help others create those alliances?

How has this contributed to the growth and development of others?

How has this contributed to your organization's success?

What resources or activities help you in pursuit of this goal?

When was the last time you used these resources in pursuit of this goal?

3. Do you recognize and value the importance of your being a strategic alliance for others to assist them in their development?

What actions have you taken to become a strategic alliance for others?

How has this contributed to your growth and development?

How has this contributed to the growth and development of others?

How has this contributed to your organization's success?

What resources or activities help you in pursuit of this goal?

When was the last time you used these resources/activities to achieve this goal?

CALL TO ACTION

Based upon your response to the Leadership Inventory, identify three (3) actions to further your continuing development and success as a leader.

Action Timetable

1.

2.

3.

SECTION III
NURTURING GROWTH

CHAPTER SEVEN

EFFECTIVE COMMUNICATION

CHAPTER 7

EFFECTIVE COMMUNICATION

> *"You have to have rain to have a rainbow!"*
>
> *—Jean Otte*

In the garden, no amount of sun, shade, soil additives, fertilizer, mulch, pruning, or weeding will result in a successful outcome without that most vital component that helps all gardens grow—water. Just as water is the most essential ingredient in the process of gardening, effective communication is the vital ingredient in the workplace. Employees require an effective communication system in the same way plants need water. It is essential for their survival. In Chapter 2, I discussed the need for the leader to create a shared vision that involves others and encourages their input and buy-in. Those same requirements apply to the process of effective communication. It must be a two-way process to be effective.

The level of an organization's (and its employees') success and growth is largely determined by the clarity of vision and the ability to communicate that vision to all levels of the organization, with a uniformly high level of understanding and commitment—top to bottom. There are numerous tools, techniques, and processes to assist leaders in these efforts. There are also numerous obstacles that present challenges. The foundation of truly effective communication within an organization is usually determined by the quality of the one-to-one, interpersonal relationships between individual leaders and those they lead.

Effective communication is defined as the transfer of information from one person to another, with clarity of understanding. In this regard, communication might seem like a very simple process. However, organization consultants and executive coaches who spend most of their time trying to help organizations and individuals improve performance and achieve greater growth usually find that faulty or ineffective communication processes are the number one issue blocking growth and success.

> "EFFECTIVE COMMUNICATION IS DEFINED AS THE TRANSFER OF INFORMATION FROM ONE PERSON TO ANOTHER, WITH CLARITY AND UNDERSTANDING."

Communication is pervasive. We are always communicating, whether we realize it or not. Sometimes organizations and individuals choose not to communicate overtly and that in itself sends a huge message to others. When asked to name one of the greatest contributors to her career, Sandy Beach Lin named strong communication and selling skills. "In my position," said Sandy, "I realize the importance of communication upwards, downwards, and across the organization. I need to be able to sell the direction of our business throughout the company, to the top leadership, and to our employees. Honing my communication skills early in my career has paid off time and again."

In his work as an executive consultant, Jack Yurish has identified the key components of communication to be: the *sender,* the *message,* and the *receiver.* "To be effective in the realm of interpersonal communications, the leader must pay significant attention to each of these components," said Jack. "At its simplest, communication is a direct transmission of information from one person (the leader) to another (the follower). However, to ensure understanding, as the definition of effective communication states, feedback becomes a must." Consequently, the process becomes circular rather than linear. Effective communication is a balance of speaking and listening.

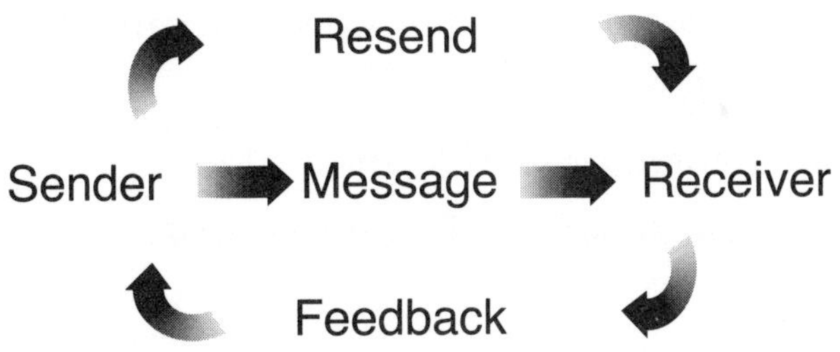

This circular and repetitive process continues until the leader is certain that the information intended to be communicated is received by the receiver, with the correct/desired level of understanding. At this point, let us examine some basics regarding each of the components.

THE SENDER

Interpersonal effectiveness requires some very basic competencies on the part of the leader. WUI regional director Amy Gonzales advises: "Essentially, leaders must demonstrate that they are capable and confident. For women, there are a number of key behaviors that are crucial to demonstrating competence." The following are some of the behaviors Amy points out to WUI participants.

- **STRONG, STILL POSTURE:** Your actions do speak louder than words. Fidgeting, head tilting, rocking, scratching, all convey lack of confidence. Powerful people keep their bodies and hands still, use deliberate gestures, and are great at maintaining composed facial expressions, no matter how flustered they may feel.
- **CONCISE WORDING:** Stop using the qualifiers that minimize impact. *Maybe, perhaps, kind of, a little, sort of* create a message of uncertainty instead of confidence. Confident people ask for what they want, do not overapologize, and get to the bottom line quickly.
- **DIRECT EYE CONTACT:** In American culture, direct eye contact conveys confidence and competence.

"DIRECT EYE CONTACT CONVEYS CONFIDENCE AND COMPETENCE."

- **Clear statements using "a voice of authority":** Think James Earl Jones! The voice of authority is slow-paced, low-pitched, with a downward inflection at the end. Women with higher-pitched voices have a disadvantage in not sounding as strong as their male counterparts. They can compensate by slowing down their rate of speech, using pauses (instead of filler words like *um, er, you know*), and practicing speaking from the diaphragm. Unfortunately, when women get passionate about an issue their voices can rise in pitch, leading to the dreaded accusation of being "shrill." Practice breathing to slow down delivery and pitch. Finally, make sure that your statements are delivered with a downward inflection (rather than a rising inflection) at the end of each sentence. Rising inflections may sound friendly, but they indicate that you are asking for approval instead of giving direct input. To practice, mentally put a period—a pause—at the end of each statement.
- **Caring:** The ability to demonstrate that you are approachable and interested in others. There are a number of key behaviors that are important to demonstrating caring. They include:
  - Use a friendly and engaging tone of voice
  - Put energy into your voice when speaking with others, instead of having a disinterested or flat tone. Speak with a smile in your voice.
  - Ask questions. If you want to be approachable, you need to engage in conversations with others.
  - Balance "report talk" with "rapport talk."
  - Use names. Remembering and using people's names is a powerful tool in conveying genuine interest.

• Appear open. People will not approach you if you do not seem to be approachable.

• Convey a message of interest and openness by smiling, direct eye contact, and open posture.

Communicating with confidence is not about emulating one model or trying to be someone you are not. It is understanding clearly who you are, and being conscious of when you are operating at your very best. We are at our best when we are feeling both competent and confident, and have the energy that makes others engage with us. A WUI participant from IBM summed it up well when she said, "I was once called a diamond in the rough. Because of that, for a long time I was trying to be someone else, someone who fit the 'mold' of a typical leader. I've realized that I can be a perfectly flawed diamond and still be successful. It's about being comfortable with me."

However, showing that you are capable and competent in speaking is only half of the communication equation. The leader must also be responsive to the other person(s). That requires skill in effective listening and responding. Both of these critical skills are usually found in leaders who possess a healthy self-concept and are able to cope with their own emotions, particularly angry feelings, and are able to express them in constructive ways. According to Dr. Richard "Rick" K. Bommelje, associate professor in the department of organizational communication at Rollins College and frequent WUI presenter: "Listening is a multifaceted behavior: active versus passive. If the awareness lightbulb is off, the person can hear, see, smell, but do it in a one-dimensional way. They may miss before the game even begins." For their book *Listening Leaders: The 10 Golden Rules to Listen, Lead & Succeed,* Rick and Dr. Lyman K. Steil interviewed 110 leaders throughout the world on the importance of listening. Many of the leaders they researched correlated listening with leading, and were open to receiving information from different sources and in different venues. "There was one [executive] who was riding up seven flights on an elevator and the person that we were interviewing was with him," said Rick. One of the executive's team members was in the elevator, and during that ride the executive "asked such probing, thoughtful questions, that he was able through listening to get a whole other perspective on the project." All this in a seven-story elevator ride! The interviews reinforced the S-I-E-R model of listening.

> "THE LISTENING ACT CONSISTS OF FOUR CONNECTED ACTIVITIES—SENSING, INTERPRETING, EVALUATING, AND RESPONDING."

"The S-I-E-R model of listening is a systematic approach for helping individuals to enhance their listening awareness and applications," said Rick. "The listening act consists of four connected activities—sensing, interpreting, evaluating, and responding. Listening is not synonymous with hearing, but good listening begins at the level of sensing the sender's message. Sensing is basic to the other three activities involved in listening—if the listener does not sense the message, he or she can do nothing further with it."

THE MESSAGE

The clarity and construction of the message, as well as the timing and environment in which it is transmitted, is a vital part of the process. Leaders must determine their own objectives in regard to the end result they wish to achieve. What goals are they striving to achieve? What actions are required on the part of the receivers of the communication?

"After the message is sensed," said Rick Bommelje, "a second activity comes into play: accurate interpretation." This is where semantic problems are encountered. "The sensitive listener," said Rick, "says 'I heard the words used by the speaker, but am I assigning a comparable meaning to them?' Effective listeners remember that 'words have no meaning—people have meaning.' The assignment of meaning to a term is an internal process (i.e., comes from inside us). And although our experiences, knowledge, and attitudes differ, we often misinterpret each other's messages while under the illusion that a common understanding has been achieved."

I advise leaders to carefully consider the goals and attitudes of those who will receive the communication, as well as those who will be affected by it. In this regard the leader has to consider the questions: What's in it for them? and What message/rationale would enable them to buy-in?

Having clarified both ends of the equation, the leader is now in a position to construct an effective message. Because the communication process involves humans on both ends of the transaction, emotions play a huge role in a leader's ability to effectively convey a message and in the receiver's ability to receive it. Timing is critical. It has often been said: "The right message at the wrong time is the wrong message." For this reason Amy Gonzales reminds workshop participants of former New York Mayor Rudy Guliani. Prior to the tragic events of September 11, 2001, Guliani's reputation was that of a tough, aggressive, and not particularly likable public figure. After September 11, 2001, Guliani became a folk hero and leader that people rallied around. Although his compassion and clear concern for the people of his city had not changed, the circumstances changed the way he was being "heard" or received.

"THE RIGHT MESSAGE AT THE WRONG TIME IS THE WRONG MESSAGE."

The leader must take this issue into consideration with every communication, especially with messages of great importance or personal impact. Excellent information delivered at the wrong time may do more harm than good. The setting in which the communication is delivered is also important. Trying to deliver an important message in an environment filled with distractions (phone, noise, passersby, and so on) will interfere with getting the job done. There are enough obstacles, some of which will be discussed later in this section, operating between the sender and receiver(s) without adding environmental distractions to the process.

The Receiver

As mentioned earlier, the receiver's needs are a critical consideration in the leader's planning of a communication. In addition to their perceptual screens, which we will cover in our discussion of feedback, there are several factors that can influence the receiver's readiness to receive the message. Among these are the communicator's position and level of authority in the organization, which can add credibility to the message but might also be threatening, depending upon the perception, maturity, and self-confidence of the receiver. Also important is the level of trust that exists between the sender and the receiver. Effective leaders always seek to understand who their audience is and what their "win" needs are.

The other issue is that of "active listening" rather than hearing. "Active listeners go beyond sensing and interpretation to another act: evaluation," said Rick Bommelje. "Here the listener decides whether or not to agree with the speaker. The evidence is weighed, fact is sorted from opinion, and judgment is rendered. Poor listeners begin this activity too soon, often hearing something they disagree with and tuning out the speaker from

"Active listeners go beyond sensing and interpretation to another act: evaluation."

that point on. When this occurs, sensing and interpretation stop—so does listening. Speakers have the right to be heard, and the best listeners delay judgment until the message is fully presented. Moreover, the best listeners work hard at developing their judgmental skills and abilities."

FEEDBACK

The next critical step for the communicator, to ensure understanding, is the solicitation of feedback from the receiver. In this regard, it is not sufficient for the communicator/sender to merely ask, "Did you understand?" A "yes" response on the part of the receiver does nothing to assure the communicator that their message was received and understood exactly as they had intended. To get helpful feedback, it is crucial that the communicator asks for specific information from the intended receiver—for example, questions like "What did you hear me say?" "Can you tell me your understanding of what I've just said?" or "How do you intend to carry out my request?" or "How do you think this will impact you and others?" All of these direct requests for the receiver to provide specific information provide the sender with the ability to assess whether or not the message has been received as intended. If it has not, the communicator has the ability to resend with additional information and/or greater clarity.

"Every effective leader realizes the critical importance of responding," said Rick Bommelje. "To respond requires the development of the ability to respond plus responsibility. The response stage of listening is especially crucial for judging the success of the listening act as a whole. This is true because the first three stages—sensing, interpreting, and evaluating—are internal acts. They take place inside of us—no one can directly observe them. Until the listener makes a concrete response, it's often difficult to determine whether the speaker has been successful in getting the point across."

As Jack Yurish stated earlier, this is why the communication process needs to be a cyclical process of sending-receiving-testing-resending, until there is a clear and mutual understanding between the sender and the receiver, the leader and their followers. This cyclical/iterative process is necessary because every person, sender and receiver, has individual perceptual screens. An individual's perceptual screen is made up of their total life experience (their upbringing, education, values, professional discipline, and many other factors). These perceptual screens condition the ways in which the individual sees, hears, and visualizes things. One person might be making reference to a fact, truth, or reality and present it as "A." The other person listening to that fact, truth, or reality, because of their perceptual screen, might hear it as "a." That is why it is critical for the communicator to solicit feedback. The communicator's attitude and response should be, "Tell me more." This will help to keep the

"TELL ME MORE."

communication process moving until mutuality of understanding is achieved.

OBSTACLES

In addition to the basic issues involved in the interaction between sender and receiver, there are numerous other issues/obstacles that impact the communication process.

THE MEANING OF WORDS

As previously mentioned, every individual has a perceptual screen. This screen applies not only to values but also to the different meanings that people give to words. A simple exercise that Jack Yurish suggests to demonstrate this point is to select a little three-letter word like "run." Share it with a group of people and ask them to give you a quick response as to what image the word *run* prompts in their mind. In response, you will get almost as many different words as you have people in the group. They will say things like *fast, jog, walk, computer, production, pantyhose,* and so on. Everyone views words in different ways. In addition, most words have more than one meaning. The confusion that often results from the different meanings that people give to words underscores the importance of obtaining feedback in the process of communicating.

DISTORTION

Another obstacle resulting from our perceptual screens is distortion. We see, hear, and visualize things through our own eyes, ears, and experiences. Very often people see and hear only what their experiences, values, and prejudices allow them to see and hear. This is often compounded when a message is passed along through several links in a communication chain. At each link in the chain, information is omitted, added, or modified based upon the perceptions of the person observing/hearing it, interpreting it, and passing it along.

Many of us have experienced this phenomenon when we played the communication party game. One person whispers a short sentence in the ear of the person sitting next to him or her. That person whispers the line in the next person's ear and so on, down the line. The last person's message rarely resembles the original. A great line was sent to me. I do not know who originally said it, I just know that it sums up distortion perfectly: "I know you believe you understand what you think I said, but I am not sure you realize that what you heard is not what I meant." A great visual definition of this occurs when one works with a graphic designer. What is in your head and what is in the artist's head may be two different things. You might ask for an illustration of a wildflower, with images of wide-open rolling plains in your head. The flower drawn by an artist with a different cultural background might be an exotic tropical wildflower found in the depths of a rain forest. One verbal description may apply to completely different visual depictions. Leaders ask for feedback to counteract distortion.

JUMPING TO CONCLUSIONS

Because of a person's experiences and prejudices, if they are not patient enough to gather all the necessary facts or to ask questions, there might be a tendency to state inference as fact. A good example is when someone sees a tow truck's flashing lights. It is natural for them to assume that the truck is going to an accident, when it might be going to pick up a stalled vehicle. Another example might be when a person of one culture observes a person of a different culture exhibiting some behavior or engaging in some activity. If the first person had a past negative experience with the other culture or has a long-standing prejudice about that culture, they might immediately jump to a conclusion and assign a negative motive to the second person's behavior or activity without taking the time to clarify the facts. Consequently, they might wind up reporting their inference as fact.

During a business trip to Japan, I gave a presentation to a group of Japanese businessmen. To my horror, almost all of them closed their eyes during the presentation. I thought they were sleeping. It was excruciating trying to get through the rest of my talk. However, once I finished, their eyes opened and they had questions to ask and praise to share. In America, closed eyes during a presentation often indicates that the speaker is less than interesting. In Japan, it is common for businessmen and -women to close their eyes while listening. It helps them focus on the one voice. Based on my past experiences, I had jumped to a conclusion. It was not until I had all the facts that I understood what was happening.

USE OF ABSTRACTIONS

Another obstacle to effective communication is the use of abstract words or jargon. Too often people get into the habit of using terms or abbreviations to convey information. This can work if everyone involved has had the same experiences or has used the same terminology. This often happens within professional disciplines or organizations. Have you ever been overwhelmed at a new job when the "old hands" carry on a conversation in your presence without recognizing your newness to the situation? You wind up asking a lot of questions, most of them being, "What does that mean?"

FAILURE TO LISTEN

If silence is golden, being able to listen during your own silence is priceless. There is a distinct difference between hearing and listening.

About seventeen years ago, Rick Bommelje realized there were problems that were occurring repeatedly, both professionally and personally, and could not figure out why. "I had a team of 14 at the time and was in a management position here at [Rollins College]. We were a good team—an awesome team—and I was unfortunately blaming other people in my mind, when it wasn't them, but it was me. As I did more reflecting, I realized it was a real listening gap

"If silence is golden, being able to listen during your own silence is priceless."

and I had no formal education in listening." In speaking about this experience, Rick reminded me that there are two outcomes to listening: either adding value or incurring a cost. By hearing and not listening, costs are incurred.

E-MAIL

The topic of e-mail is a source of many discussions in the WUI program. Using e-mail has become the preferred method of communicating for most people in today's business world. However, e-mails are the cause of many communications disconnects in business today. They do not rely on the traditional speaking-and-listening model of communication. And, unlike letters, they are often "shot out" without a second thought. They incorporate many of the obstacles previously listed: the meaning of words, distortion, jumping to conclusions.

When used incorrectly, e-mail has been the root of many problems. My personal caveat is that e-mail is an excellent tool for conveying information quickly and efficiently and for responding to questions requiring very little explanation. It is not, however, and should not be, a tool used as a sole source for detailed explanations. It should be accompanied by a phone call or face-to-face meeting to ensure that the reader comprehends the sender's intended message. It certainly should not be used to have "a conversation" that could be misinterpreted by the receiver.

In face-to-face communication, we read body language. In e-mails, colors and fonts take on special meaning. Words in caps may indicate anger to some, but may be a mode of differentiation for others. Red may show irritation, but might be a way to make one sentence stand out from another. Depending upon the mood of the receiver, an e-mail about a controversial subject may be read in an "annoyed" tone in the reader's head, even though it was jotted down by a levelheaded sender.

"IF YOU DON'T HAVE SOMETHING NICE TO SAY, DON'T WRITE IT IN AN E-MAIL."

If you don't have something nice to say, don't write it in an e-mail. Remember, it is so much easier to circulate an e-mail than it is a hard copy. Within seconds, a poorly thought out or misunderstood e-mail can be in the hands of hundreds. I am personally appalled at e-mails that clearly reflect a person's dissatisfaction or ones that sound accusatory. I encourage effective communication involving speaking and active listening—neither of which is possible via e-mail.

I am also concerned about e-mails of this nature that are copied to others. This type of communication process is, to say the least, a passive-aggressive behavior that does not lend itself to effective communication. When I have received this type of e-mail I immediately respond by asking to speak with the individual.

I know of countless occasions when I and others have been angered or insulted by an e-mail, and in many instances it was not the intent of the sender. Nothing can truly replace the process of being able to hear another person and have the opportunity to respond through talking and listening.

OLD-FASHIONED ETIQUETTE

I want to talk briefly about the subject of business etiquette. In this day and age, when we are so reliant on technology, voice mail, e-mail, etc., I would highly recommend taking the time to do some things that may be old-fashioned but are still very highly valued. For example, don't send an e-mail to say thank-you for something that someone has done for you—send a handwritten note. It is far more personal and has far more impact today than receiving an e-mail among the 500 other e-mails that a person has to look through. Send a personal, hand-written note saying thank-you; send a letter out to a team or a group of individuals that you've worked with, just acknowledging how much you appreciate what they've done, and copy that to their boss. If you see that someone is being promoted or given an opportunity for a new assignment, anything of that nature, send that person a note, circle the announcement, whatever it takes—do something very personal to congratulate them and tell them that you wish them the very best and ask if there is anything you can do to be helpful. Or if you see that there is an article in a magazine or newspaper, send it along to people that you think might have an interest and put your comments on it. If there is something about your company that highlights it in a positive manner, anything of that nature—just taking the time to do those small but very significant things are the types of savvy moments that you need to take and make the time for.

THE VIRTUAL OFFICE

With more people working out of home offices or working in offices separated by thousands of miles, we do not always have the opportunity to work face-to-face with colleagues. Part of communication is body language. As discussed earlier, a lot is expressed by a shrug of the shoulders, a smile, the raising of the eyebrows. In her book *Virtual Leadership*, executive coach Val Williams offers several strategies for how to be a strong leader in a virtual world. For example, during conference calls a leader's voice becomes the chief tool for influencing others.

Val's "6 Tips for an Effective Virtual Oral Presentation":

- **TONE AND INFLECTION OF VOICE:** Tone should fluctuate and not be monotone. Does your tone communicate strong leadership? On your next conference call, set up a portable audiotape in the background to evaluate your own tone for yourself.
- **VOLUME OF VOICE:** Strong leaders have good volume to their voice. Check with the audience on how well you are being heard.
- **SPEED OF VOICE:** Hesitations in speaking make a leader sound tentative. Speaking too slow loses the audience. Speaking too fast makes it sound like you cannot wait to get "leading" over with.

- **Confidence:** Your voice should communicate confidence. In the virtual world this means your voice should project energy. Energy in your voice can be felt and influences people.
- **Check for Understanding:** When speaking on a teleconference, be sure to check in with the audience frequently, since you cannot see them. For example, ask: "Does what I just said make sense?"
- **Laser It:** Speak concisely. Get to the point. Busy senior executives do not have a lot of time for endless detail. Stick to overall strategy.

Actions Speak Louder than Words

Take the time to communicate. Leaders who take the initiative to recognize others for their contributions make a strong nonverbal communication. Their actions speak volumes. Not only do their words have a message, but their actions say, "I care."

In her book *Work Would Be Great if It Weren't for the People*, author Ronna Lichtenberg offers a tongue-in-cheek look at those managers who would far rather "just do their jobs" than have to interact with the people they work with. In reality, a successful leader knows the way to get the job done is with commitment and through others. If a leader does not pay attention to the people-side of the business and focuses almost continuously on task, it can and will result in a negative outcome. The leader's ability to communicate appreciation is a make-it-

or-break-it point in the success of many organizations. It is essential that each individual, whether a newly hired employee or senior employee, feels valued and recognized for their contributions. When they do not, they often leave the organization.

Recognition for employee contributions is the key to high-performing teams. There are so many ways in which that can be done and it does not have to be time-consuming or costly. Years ago I learned from a wonderful manager at McDonald's how important it is to make employees feel valued and saw for myself how that contributes to employees wanting to be great team players. Every morning that he was in town, he held a five-minute stand-up meeting with everyone in his department. He asked how everyone was doing, recognized special days such as birthdays and anniversaries, and thanked everyone for their efforts from the day before. He shared business "news of the day," making all the employees feel included and valued. We had weekly project report meetings and monthly team meetings at which we were encouraged to discuss anything we felt needed to be addressed.

In the WUI programs, one of the most important aspects of the success of the learning experience is the environment created by the program facilitators and the participants and mentors. Everyone is encouraged to express their opinions and share their successes or concerns. One of the highlights of the program each month is what we call sharing "noteworthy news," or as I like to describe it, "refrigerator moments." I explain that we need to remember how excited many of us were as children when we ran home to show our parents the picture we had painted or the report card we were proud of, and our mum or dad would post it on the refrigerator for all to see and admire. I still have many of my two sons' early "refrigerator masterpieces," which I love to look at to recall their early achievements and how proud we were!

When the women stand up and share their "noteworthy news" and the group applauds and congratulates them, it is like watching flowers turn from buds into beautiful blooms. Many of the participants have said this is one of the most positive aspects of the program. We also encourage the participants to remember to create those moments in their individual workplaces for others with whom they work. Long after the women have graduated from the program, many continue to meet either in person or virtually. One of their agenda items is to share their noteworthy news.

> "THE LEADER'S ABILITY TO COMMUNICATE APPRECIATION IS A MAKE-IT-OR-BREAK-IT POINT IN THE SUCCESS OF MANY ORGANIZATIONS."

Recognition is as necessary to people as sunlight and water are to plants, and so often leaders go about the business of business without recognizing the importance of this key aspect of their role. I can remember when my NCR team had to work many long hours and sometimes weekends as we rolled out a new program for customers nationwide. Taking the time to recognize those employees was essential to keeping them motivated and making sure that, no matter what, they were encouraged to "down tools" and go home and relax and reenergize whenever possible.

In business we all know there are times when we are asked to work longer hours, and an employee who knows that he or she will be given recognition for those efforts will almost always be willing to do so.

Encouraging and supporting employees to continue their professional development is one way leaders demonstrate their interest in employees and is one of the key factors in creating an environment of value. Listening to employees and giving them opportunities to contribute their ideas and, above all, letting them take responsibility for their role is also essential to their growth.

"RECOGNITION IS AS NECESSARY TO PEOPLE AS SUNLIGHT AND WATER ARE TO PLANTS."

When offering recognition and setting requirements during performance reviews, it is especially important for leaders to communicate effectively. Leaders must be clear about their message and listen to employees to ensure that the message is received correctly.

If, for example, the leader sets requirements regarding expectations, timelines, or costs of a particular project, it is essential that the employee be given the opportunity to question those requirements. It is also essential that he or she be asked probing, open-ended questions that will allow the leader to determine if what is being asked is fully understood. If that employee is then required to convey those requirements to others, the leader needs to have the employee demonstrate how he or she intends to deliver the message.

During a performance review, when the leader gives an employee feedback on a performance issue, it is important for the leader to listen to the employee to determine what the employee believes has contributed to this issue. The leader should then ask the employee how he or she plans to improve before giving advice on what the employee can do. It is also very effective when requesting an employee make improvements in certain areas to give the employee a list of resources he or she could utilize to improve in those areas. If the employee needs to be more effective in making presentations or in financial expertise, give him or her a list of books, materials, workshops, and seminars available through the company.

SUMMARY

You might be wondering, "How does anything ever get accomplished?" or thinking "With all of the things that can get in the way of communication, it's amazing that anything ever gets done." Certainly, there is a lot to think about when it comes to communicating effectively, and the reality is that in this treatment of the subject, we have only scratched the surface, so to speak. When it comes to effective interpersonal communication, the leader has to remember that it is a one-to-one process. If you focus on the basic key components and make them a fundamental part of your skill set, you will effectively cover the important steps in communicating. So let us summarize the key components:

- **THE SENDER**—Know your objective for the communication. Express yourself clearly. Be flexible and responsive to the other person(s).

- **THE RECEIVER**—Know your audience. Be aware of the receiver's attitude and "win" needs. Work to build trust.

- **THE MESSAGE**—Ensure the clarity of the message. Avoid abstract words and jargon. Consider proper timing and setting for the communication.

- **FEEDBACK**—Never assume. Test for understanding. Ask specific questions. Seek specific answers. Remember that everyone has a perceptual screen.

- **RESEND**—Create a cyclical/iterative process until mutuality of understanding is achieved.

I'd like to add one last word about recognition. Winston Churchill said: "Courage is what it takes to stand up and speak; courage is also what it takes to sit down and listen." Communication plays a role in every aspect of leadership. If told that I could use it only in one manner, it would be to give recognition to others. It does take a lot of courage to speak and to lis-

> "COURAGE IS WHAT IT TAKES TO STAND UP AND SPEAK; COURAGE IS ALSO WHAT IT TAKES TO SIT DOWN AND LISTEN."

ten—especially when the communication is delivering an unwanted message. By recognizing your employees and colleagues, you are acknowledging and rewarding this courage. They had to stand up and speak, and sit down and listen, in order to achieve success.

If you cover the basics well, you will be able to establish a highly effective two-way communication process that benefits you, the others with whom you interact, and the organization. In the next chapter we will look at how to sustain the growth and development of individuals and the organization.

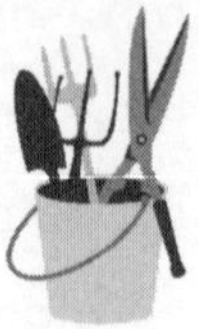

LEADERSHIP INVENTORY

1. Do you recognize and value the importance of creating an environment that fosters open, honest, two-way communication?

What actions have you taken to create this environment?

How has this contributed to your growth and development?

How has this contributed to the growth and development of others?

How has this contributed to your organization's success?

What resources/activities help you in pursuit of this goal?

When was the last time you used these resources/activities in pursuit of this goal?

2a. Do you recognize and value the importance of the "sender" having primary responsibility in an effective communication process?

What actions have you taken to fulfill this responsibility?

How has this contributed to your growth and development?

How has this contributed to the growth and development of others?

How has this contributed to your organization's success?

What resources or activities help you assess how well you are achieving this goal?

When was the last time you used these resources in pursuit of this goal?

2b. Do you recognize and value the importance of listening and receiving feedback?

What actions have you taken to use and assess those skills?

How has this contributed to your growth and development?

How has this contributed to the growth and development of others?

How has this contributed to your organization's success?

What resources or activities help you in pursuit of this goal?

When was the last time you used these resources/activities in pursuit of this goal?

3. Do you recognize and value the importance of providing appropriate recognition in the development of others?

What actions have you taken that demonstrate your commitment to the recognition process?

How has this contributed to the growth and development of others?

How has this contributed to your organization's success?

What resources/activities help you in pursuit of this goal?

When was the last time you used these resources/activities in pursuit of this goal?

CALL TO ACTION

Based upon your response to the Leadership Inventory, identify three (3) actions to further your continuing development and success as a leader.

Action	Timetable
1.	
2.	
3.	

SECTION IV
PRUNING & WEEDING

CHAPTER EIGHT

PRUNING & WEEDING

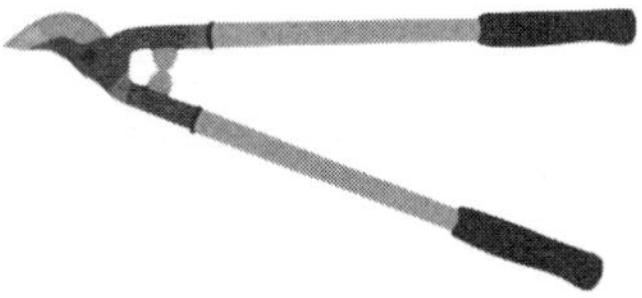

CHAPTER 8

PRUNING AND WEEDING

> *"The more you garden the more you grow."*
>
> *—The Book of Outdoor Gardening*

Peter Drucker once said: "The only things that evolve by themselves in an organization are disorder, friction and malperformance." The same is true in gardening. Without pruning, weeding, or transplanting, even the most beautiful plants can become ugly. In both the garden and in business, these processes should occur on a constant basis rather than when an obvious problem has arisen. It should be a form of preventative maintenance, ensuring the growth and development of employees and the workplace.

Most successful organizations routinely work toward streamlining their processes and reducing costs. In many instances, that means restructuring, reorganizing, downsizing, and, as some call it, rightsizing. In gardening, this process takes place in the form of pruning and weeding. Plants are pruned to encourage proper growth. For example, in the winter, just as in slow periods in business, plants are cut back in the same way employees may be to save the strength of the organization. As with gardeners, sometimes organization leaders must "weed" to remove problematic growth. Leaders may also need to transplant talented employees from one area to another.

PRUNING

As every great gardener knows, it is essential to regularly prune or deadhead many of the plants and flowers in the garden. The pruning process requires great patience and a clear understanding of each plant's and flower's needs. The correct pruning will reward growth.

There is no one-size-fits-all gardening tool to accomplish this task. Imagine going into a beautiful herbaceous border with garden shears and lopping off the tops of all the plants and flowers in one fell swoop. Imagine the disastrous outcome. Each plant has a specific requirement for pruning. Cutting straight off the top is not the solution.

In Chapter 1, I spoke about the many employees who fail to receive feedback from their managers. Unappreciated and unrecognized employees are one of the greatest problems in the workplace. As plants in a garden, they might grow out of control or wither. Whenever Michele Coleman Mayes stepped outside her comfort zone, she would look for new mentors or advisors who were "wired and invested" in her success. "I turned to those individuals regularly not just for advice, but for a read on how I was progressing," said Michele. "You cannot fix what you are not aware of and I know that it is not possible to do a self-critique and catch everything." Like plants, people need to be constantly monitored and fertilized. In business, the fertilizer is feedback. And, as in the garden, it should be applied more than once a year.

> "YOU CANNOT FIX WHAT YOU ARE NOT AWARE OF AND I KNOW THAT IT IS NOT POSSIBLE TO DO A SELF-CRITIQUE AND CATCH EVERYTHING."

PERFORMANCE FEEDBACK

One of the most critical tasks for a leader is to provide effective performance feedback. Unfortunately, it is an area that many leaders avoid. Rosina Racioppi, who spent many years in human resources in corporate America, has found that although most managers are well skilled in their "technical" area of responsibility, be it accounting, engineering, or marketing, when it comes to managing the performance of their staff, they falter. "Often there is a fear of hurting the individual's feelings and just not being comfortable themselves with having this discussion," said Rosina. "Closing their eyes is a way of shortchanging people," said Susan Sobbott. "While you think that you are the only one paying the price, you are not. It's that person's colleagues and employees who are paying the price. When you have a poor performer, it typically affects a dozen people. It also takes your time in a way your time is not meant to be spent." As with weeds in the garden, leaders will have more work if they ignore the weeds when they appear than if they immediately take care of them.

> "CLOSING THEIR EYES IS A WAY OF SHORTCHANGING PEOPLE."

One of the most caring and productive acts any manager can do is to provide their staff with performance feedback—to reinforce the things that they are doing well and to discuss ways to improve areas needing attention. As I discussed in Chapter 7, recognition is a vital tool for leaders. Rosina emphasizes that "it is important to remember that when people come to work, they want to contribute their best." If they are not, it may be because they need assistance in better understanding how to contribute their best. A leader must speak to an employee to learn if the root of the poor performance is the leader's responsibility. Perhaps the leader is not providing enough support or did not offer the needed training for the employee. The employee may be in a job that is too small for his or her spirit and may not be interested in it. It is very difficult to give one's best performance if the job is one the employee feels no passion about. If you are trying to sing grand opera in a country-and-western bar, neither you nor the audience are going to enjoy the experience.

"One choice is to assess the person's strengths," said Susan. "Give them things to do that suit them and they become a better performer. I compare these types of employees to marathon runners who we ask to run sprints. They are not very good, because they're not really fast, but they've got great endurance. Well, stop making them do sprints and give them something that requires endurance. Organizations, particularly large organizations, want people who are good at a lot of things. The problem is that when you have an organization full of people who are good at a lot of things, nobody's great at anything. And it is hard for an organization to be great if you've got a lot of good people. Typically, people who are great at some things aren't so great at other things. How many athletes do you know who play five sports? People tend to be great at something, so the trick is being able to figure out what that something is and then letting them flourish within that."

The following process is one that Rosina has coached many managers on through the WUI program:

- Be clear about what the performance issue is
- Create solutions to the performance issue with the employee
- Set clear expectations of performance
- Conduct follow-up meetings with employees to monitor progress

Let's review those four steps:

Be clear about what the performance issue is. It is important to articulate the performance issue in a clear fashion so the individual understands what they are doing incorrectly. Since managers are uncomfortable giving this type of feedback, some may sandwich the feedback in between other conversations with the hope that the employee will just "get it." This rarely works. Effective feedback needs to be clear. If an employee's monthly report is consistently late and includes inaccuracies, the employee needs to be told that his or her credibility with the organization is being affected.

> "TELL ME AND I FORGET. TEACH ME AND I REMEMBER. INVOLVE ME AND I LEARN."

CREATE SOLUTIONS TO THE PERFORMANCE ISSUE WITH THE EMPLOYEE. Most managers fail to see the importance of this very simple step. As Benjamin Franklin said: "Tell me and I forget. Teach me and I remember. Involve me and I learn." By telling an employee the solution to a performance issue, a leader is not inspiring commitment on the employee's part to follow the suggestions. By exploring various solutions with the employee and together determining the solutions that address the performance issue, the employee will be more committed to take action. The employee must be made to feel he or she is a part of the process. Although the leader will work with the employee, it is the employee's responsibility to make the change. The leader can only further impede the employee's progress by doing everything for him or her.

The following story was shared with me as an illustration of this point. A man was looking at a butterfly attempting to emerge from its cocoon. As the man watched, he was moved as he observed the butterfly struggling to break free of the cocoon. Having a great deal of sympathy for its plight, the man decided to help the poor butterfly. He gently and carefully opened up the cocoon, thereby reducing the effort and struggle for the butterfly. In his kindness, the man did not realize that he had actually caused the butterfly great harm and the butterfly was not able to fly. The butterfly needed to go through the process of emerging from the cocoon without aid in order to gain the strength and skills needed to fly. In WUI's the FEW (Forums for Executive Women) program, executive coach Val Williams and I coined the phrase "butterfly coaching." We counsel the group to listen and question each other rather than jumping in with solutions as other people are sharing their concerns. It is so very easy to tell others how to do things, isn't it? Many of us are very quick to want to fix it for other people and give them the benefit of our great wisdom, when in fact they need to find their own solution. This goes back to the John Gardner quote: "All too often we're giving people cut flowers, when we should be teaching them to grow their own plants."

Set clear expectations of performance. Help the employee understand the consequences of not meeting performance expectations. If an employee continues having problems meeting the expectations, the employee needs to know that the leader wants to hear what the continued problem is—that, up to a point, the leader is willing to work with the employee as long as a line of effective communication remains open. The leader might find that it is the expectations that are the problem. They may be set too high or too low.

Conduct follow-up meetings with employees to monitor progress. This will keep employees on track and provide managers an opportunity to provide support as needed. One method I've used to offer employees an assist out of the mud is to give them a stretch assignment. With help, guidance, and support, the employee can become revitalized by being given something that is more challenging than previous work assignments.

It is also helpful to assign poor performers to mentors—individuals from within the department or from other departments who could be helpful to them. It is interesting to see what happens when you put an employee who is having problems with an employee who is highly motivated. The stronger employee helps the "weaker" employee stand tall and take on a more positive attitude.

With the support of the leader, employees can get back on track and become valuable contributors again. However, as shown in the story about the butterfly, they must "be the change" if they are to succeed. Others cannot do it for them.

When dealing with employees who have not been stellar contributors, it is important to sit down with them and ask them what they believe is going on with them and their job. What are they feeling about their contribution? Get their side of the story before you start any dialogue about corrective action. Their perception of their performance may be different from your perception.

Oftentimes in these dialogues, the leader will find out that there is something going on with the employee outside the work environment that has created a problem. It may not be something the employee has shared, even though it is inhibiting them and causing them to be distracted. I had one colleague with a manager who went from being highly effective to contributing very little in a short period. My colleague sat down with him to find out what was going on. The manager's wife was ill and it was weighing heavily on his mind. Because he had always been a valued contributor to the organization, the manager was offered more assistance with his workload and flex-time to spend with his wife. My colleague also helped the manager find support groups to help him and his wife. In the garden, this manager might have been any of a number of plants that stopped flourishing. Instead of pulling it out, the gardener prunes the plant and waits to see if new growth will follow. As with the gardener, the leader sees the potential for new growth.

Within my own organization, WUI, one of our high-performing team members, who had consistently performed her job function in an above-average manner, began to show definite signs of not meeting her job requirements. Errors were occurring that, left unattended, could have resulted in severe financial implications. Upon review, we determined that this individual's workload had increased almost 100 percent as our organization grew, yet I had not been paying close attention. This individual, typical of so many achievement-oriented women, was attempting to keep up without complaint and had not asked for the help she clearly needed.

The lessons we learned were:

- As the leader, I had to recognize that I needed to have someone else take responsibility for overlooking some of the job functions and the people who performed those functions. It is important for leaders to accept that, as responsibilities increase, there are times when they want to hold on to things—even if it is not in the best interest of the organization to do it!

- As the person doing the work, it was important to have this individual feel much more comfortable letting us know the status of her workload and asking for the help she needed. She would not be judged as incapable but rather as helping to make our support processes better through her input and recommendations.
- It became very clear that her workload was far too much for any one person to perform well. As a result, the process was divided between two individuals and is now truly outstanding. In making that decision, we asked our team member to train the new person. That resulted not only in her regaining her self-confidence in her abilities but has also resulted in her being able to perform her duties in an even more effective and productive manner, and in her being able to make ongoing process improvements.

IDENTIFY THE PROBLEM

Leaders must first determine whether their employee knows he or she has a problem. Oftentimes people get into habits that they are unaware of until somebody has the courage and the concern to discuss it with them. These habits could be related to poor decision-making skills or the wrong style for conflict management. They may be the result of poor confidence and the Imposter Syndrome, which was discussed in Chapter 3. Sometimes being told that their behaviors are not in the best interest of their career or the company is enough to resolve the problem. If the problematic behavior continues, a leader might find that he or she has a poor performer on staff.

DECISION-MAKING AND RISK-TAKING

"The puck is in the net." This was one of my husband Ron's favorite sayings. At some point, the only option is to move forward with the game. Individuals who fail to make timely decisions miss tremendous opportunities when their indecisiveness holds up projects or other people. Time is ticking away and they don't realize that others are "scoring" while they are still reviewing their strategy options. In Chapter 3, I discussed the pitfalls of perfectionism. Some people have to be certain they have it perfect. They spend an enormous amount of time collecting information on which they will base their decision. Unfortunately, the quest for perfection can lead to missed deadlines and lost opportunities. As Susan B. Anthony once said: "Cautious, careful people, always casting about to preserve their reputations . . . can never effect a reform."

> "THE PUCK IS IN THE NET."

Oftentimes there is tremendous discomfort connected with making a decision because it could lead to a poor outcome. So, people need to ask themselves: What is the very worst thing that could happen to me because of this decision? How many people have been immediately staked to an anthill out on the front lawn when they made a bad decision?

"Leadership skills are very much enhanced through making tough decisions," said Sandy Beach Lin. "When I began my tenure as division president of a large commercial vehicle brake manufacturer, it became clear very quickly that the business was at an inflection point—either it needed to receive a very large infusion of capital to design new products, or it needed to be divested from the company. It was clear to me that the best route for the business was to be divested to a company that would invest in growth and the people of the division. Within my first 30 days on the job, I was before the chairman of the corporation proposing that the division be divested. This meant significant changes for our employees, not to mention my family, as we knew this would probably entail yet another move. That said, it was the right decision. The division was eventually sold, it is now growing with new products, and the employees are happy being with a company that is investing in them."

The challenge for leaders is to help employees become comfortable with the fact that not every decision is going to be the all-time best decision, and that few are going to be easily made. Employees need to hear from you that not every decision or every risk you ever took was in the best interest of the company. It is realistic and it is how the real world of business runs. The fact is, oftentimes people are paralyzed into not making any decision for fear of it not being perfect. So let us look at what can be done, perhaps, to minimize the risk. The ability to make tough decisions is respected by employees and colleagues alike. Vicki Lostetter, vice president of human resources at Coca-Cola, used to work with Sandy. When asked to comment on Sandy's leadership style, she mentioned "the ability to make tough decisions, and the ability to carry out the implications of a tough decision with heart."

Share your decision-making process with your employees. Discuss how you have made a decision, why you made the decision, the steps you went through to make the decision. Leaders must help employees discover the areas in which they have the greatest discomfort in making decisions. For example, an employee may be outstanding at making decisions that involve financial expenditures or work flow, process flow, etc., but perhaps may not be as good at making decisions about who to hire and who to terminate. If you begin to really look at where it is that the employee has the most discomfort, it is often best to match them with someone who excels in their area of discomfort. A leader can help establish an alliance, giving the employee the opportunity to talk with people that they've identified as outstanding in this area, and learn from them.

In one of the departments I used to run, I had the people that reported to me create a budget based on the information I provided them from the year before. I had them create a budget for the department even though it was not their responsibility. I would review it with them to show them what my budget was actually going to look like and what the final budget was going to look like after it was approved. It was an opportunity for them to gain confidence and practice making decisions within areas they were uncomfortable. After making their decisions, they could review what the actual budget was and how it played out through the year—and whether their decisions would have been good or bad.

In the 1990s, San Antonio, Texas, was home to a true "hot war" between the Rupert Murdoch–owned *San Antonio Express-News* and the Hearst Corporation–owned *San Antonio Light*. Both newspapers were profitable and rocked along with always escalating competitive initiatives. Then came the Texas recession, during which literally all newspapers lost one-third of their ad revenues.

It was in this context that the *San Antonio Express-News* imported a consumer game from England called Wingo. Bingo-like cards were mailed to every home throughout southwest Texas. Consumers matched the numbers on the cards with numbers published daily in the newspaper. The prizes offered helped boost the sales of the Sunday paper, which was the newspaper's real objective of the promotion. This boosted circulation numbers and created an advertiser perception of momentum and "winning" the newspaper battle.

The *San Antonio Light* offered a series of consumer promotions, but its weekly market research indicated that the Wingo game was the single most popular element in the market and was drawing a larger audience each week. The *San Antonio Light* was discouraged and sensed the prospect of losing the market battle because, in that recession environment, advertisers were increasingly choosing only one newspaper for their ads. That was the environment Robert J. Danzig, the nationwide head of the Hearst Newspaper Group, entered when he visited San Antonio for a few days of creative brainstorming. At the end of the first day of his visit, the *San Antonio Light* editor, Ted Warmbold, asked if the group could stop at a museum where his curator friend had just launched a new exhibit of Mexican folk art. As the group walked through the exhibit, the curator and local community relations director explained the pieces of art.

When the group came to what looked like a gauze-covered board game, with carved elements adhered to it, the community relations director explained that the board depicted Lotteria, which was a Mexican bingo that Mexican Americans grew up playing with their families.

At the time, San Antonio's population was 56% Mexican American. Bob turned to the *San Antonio Light*'s publisher and said, "Lotteria is our new game." Within weeks, the *San Antonio Light* launched the game. It became an instant success—vastly more popular than the competitor's Wingo. The tide turned and the *San Antonio Light*'s circulation numbers and ad revenue soared. Not much later, Hearst acquired the Rupert Murdoch–owned *San Antonio Express-News*.

"You may be disappointed if you fail," said Beverly Sills, "but you are doomed if you don't try." This is the perfect example of an opportunity that could have been missed if Bob

"YOU MAY BE DISAPPOINTED IF YOU FAIL, BUT YOU ARE DOOMED IF YOU DON'T TRY."

had not taken a risk and made an immediate decision. It also shows that not all the research in the world will ensure a winning idea.

"The ability to make the tough decisions does not come easily to either gender, although for women it carries a special challenge," said Jill Kanin-Lovers. "If you don't visibly make the tough decisions, you can be accused of being indecisive and, worse still, 'scatterbrained.' Both are considered typical female flaws. On the other hand, if you are too aggressive on decisions, particularly on firing poor performers, you can be accused of being rash (code for emotional) or even 'bitchy.' Neither are admirable traits." Making decisions requires risk, the confidence to take risks, and basic background on the issue at hand. Although there is no 100 percent way to ensure that a decision will be the right one, a mix of basic background information and confidence helps the odds.

CONFLICT MANAGEMENT

Another area of concern for many employees is how to deal with workplace conflict and negotiation to achieve a mutually beneficial outcome. Leaders can help employees become more comfortable in these areas.

"YOU BRING YOURSELF TO CONFLICT."

"You bring yourself to conflict." That phrase has been a big "aha moment" for the women attending conflict management workshops given by WUI regional director Deb Hornell. In Chapter 7, I discussed distortion and how it is an obstacle to effective communication. The same holds true with conflict management. In her workshops, Deb discusses the power of perception and its impact on how we "see" a situation. We see, hear, and visualize things through our own eyes, ears, and experiences. Our past experiences and values affect how we interpret events and can distort the real picture.

When dealing with employees who have one model for conflict management, leaders have to remember that an employee's behavior is often based on more than the present conflict. Leaders have to remind employees that this behavior puts them at a disadvantage. Others know that the employee may be combative or overly passive, and use that to their benefit. Once individuals "become more strategic about analyzing and managing conflict, they'll be more purposeful about choosing an approach in a given situation," said Deb. "Don't automatically fall into a pattern of behavior just because it's what you always do. Think about the consequences of a particular approach. If you always avoid conflict, what happens in the long term for the business, for your working relationships, and for the perception of you?"

Deb suggests looking at the situation from the other party's point of view to widen the perspective. "Think about how they might describe what's going on currently and what they want to happen. Take the risk to start a dialogue with the other party to discuss the situation and together identify potential options. Not only can it result in solutions that you might not have considered, you can enhance your working relationships with others."

The inability to effectively negotiate often holds women back from reaching their full potential. Lee Miller, managing director of NegotiationPlus.com and coauthor, with his daughter, Jessica, of *A Woman's Guide to Successful Negotiating*, has identified four basic negotiating styles that he uses when he teaches and coaches clients in the art of negotiation. They are Competitive, Accommodating, Avoiding and Collaborative. "A person with a competitive style is focused primarily on outcome. An accommodating style focuses primarily on the relationship—in other words, you will sacrifice your goals for the sake of the relationship. Avoiding is exactly what it sounds like—you hope that you will get what you want by avoiding the topic and hoping things will ultimately work out the way you would like. A collaborative style is one where you work with the other party to reach a balance where you achieve a good outcome while maintaining a positive relationship," said Lee. "Everyone exhibits some or all of these tendencies in terms of how they negotiate. They value outcome and relationship differently and thereby create their own style.

"THE INABILITY TO EFFECTIVELY NEGOTIATE OFTEN HOLDS WOMEN BACK FROM REACHING THEIR FULL POTENTIAL."

"As a general rule, every individual has their own negotiating style," said Lee. "I have an assessment tool that I use to identify an individual's negotiating style, but in general women tend to be more relationship focused and men tend to be more outcome focused. Therefore, men tend to be more 'competitive' and women tend to be more 'accommodating' or 'collaborative.'" Problems occur when people try to negotiate using styles other than their own. "Women whose natural negotiating style is competitive can usually do that well," said Lee. "The real problem for women whose real style is more collaborative or accommodating is that they adopt a competitive style because that is the way they think they should negotiate. It doesn't work because people see through you when you are not genuine." Women who attempt to do that often are labeled in negative terms. But women who have a competitive style and know how to use it effectively can pull it off. "They pull it off with humor," said Lee. "They pull it off because it is who they are. There are a number of women with competitive negotiating styles who do it well because that's their natural style, but most women don't have that as their natural style." No one is born a great negotiator. Negotiating is a skill that needs to be learned. Too often women believe that requires learning to negotiate "like a man" or not negotiating at all. What it really requires is to learn how to use your own style to negotiate effectively with people who may have different negotiating styles.

"It is true that you might have different demeanors when it comes to different environments," said Michele Coleman Mayes. "Yet, the essence of who you are is always discernible. Life is too short to go around masquerading, besides it's obvious to anyone taking the time to look closely that you are doing just that. I have been able to confront some very difficult situations because the person on the other side believed I was being sincere."

In Chapter 3, I discussed the style issues I overcame through the help of Jack Yurish and my experiences at ECL. Leaders should work with employees so they are aware of the different styles and encourage them to assess their performance reviews to determine if style is an issue. If style is an issue, leaders must encourage them to work within their own style, rather than a model of what they think is expected of them. Many women mimicked the style of men because that had been the business model for years. Leaders can help their employees by having them practice their skills and volunteering to coach them. Employees should also be referred to opportunities within their organizations to attend workshops on the topic or register for external programs.

> "Life is too short to go around masquerading."

At the end of the day, leaders should ask themselves and encourage employees to ask themselves what they bring to conflict. How can you broaden your perspective to see the situation from another perspective and evaluate multiple options? Which approach makes the most sense for a given situation? One of Lee's main points to negotiation that everyone can use despite individual style is "Try to develop a relationship first because it is hard to say no to someone you like." This is often the best way to establish a positive climate when going into a high-stress negotiation.

DOWNSIZING

Sometimes it is an organization and not simply an individual within the organization that needs to be pruned. It has to be recognized that this is a very difficult time for organizations. Oftentimes when there is a major reorganization or downsizing, employees are let go very quickly. There are instances when employees are asked to pack up their desks and leave within an hour of the announcement. During one particularly difficult period at NCR, I was required to downsize one of my divisions. Although the company had requested that it be done quickly and the employees be told to leave immediately, I made the decision to give those laid off the opportunity to talk to and say good-bye to their friends and colleagues, rather than being hustled out the door as though they had committed some crime. Then I called together all the remaining employees to reassure them that they were going to continue as part of the team. I emphasized how much I needed their support and how much I needed them to know that I was there to help them in any way they felt was necessary.

Within a few days of this reorganization, we had everyone look at their department's goals and what needed to be achieved. We examined the processes for achieving the goals, asking if they were essential to providing the kind of service that we wanted to provide customers, or were they perhaps helpful internally but not absolutely necessary. Because everyone was involved in that process and had the opportunity to give input, we redesigned many of the processes that were outdated and found many opportunities to improve, and in some instances eliminate, work. For the remaining staff, this was a positive approach, as they were not going to be asked to take on the work of those that had been laid off.

Organizations have, for the most part, attempted to put in place a process that helps those being downsized from their jobs—everything from outplacement to attempting to help employees with counseling as they deal with the ramifications of job loss. There are all types of supports, from dealing with getting résumés updated to actual job placement. It is important for a leader to manage this process and, in particular, deal with the feelings, concerns, shock, and sometimes anger, of the employees being let go. Most organizations do provide support for the leader and attempt to assist them in managing this very difficult process.

"Making the tough calls regarding employee layoffs or terminations is one of the most challenging aspects of leadership," said Sandy Beach Lin. "This is clearly an area where the leader must take time to get it right. When it comes to employee terminations for lack of performance, once I have exhausted the means available to help the employee improve his or her performance (coaching, performance improvement plans, etc.), it is best to quickly move the employee out of the company. The same goes for larger-scale layoffs. In my career, these types of layoffs or facility closings have all had a solid business case behind the decision. Even with fact-based explanations for the layoffs, it is vital to remember that you are affecting people's lives significantly. At the end of the day, the tough call to reduce head count becomes a practical decision—the really tough part, and one of great importance, is ensuring that the plans are executed with the most care and concern possible for the employees."

It is my personal belief that there is no easy way to achieve this goal. It is vital that leaders be present and visible to the employees and not attempt to conduct business as usual within the next few days of any kind of reorganization.

I must add here that in several instances when I was part of a major reorganization and downsizing, there was no doubt that the redesign resulted in a much more streamlined and effective product. The whole process reminds me of an experience I had during a vacation in South Africa. As we were traveling up Table Mountain in the cable car, the guide explained that at various times of the year there were tremendous fires on the mountainside. The fires are allowed to burn because they are a force of nature that clears out the underbrush, nourishes the soil, and makes way for new, lush growth on the mountain. This might seem like a harsh analogy to business, but reorganizations and downsizings—whatever you want to call them—are harsh. Although business is not supposed to be personal, it is. It is difficult to see people go. The process is difficult for the entire organization, but at the end, the "fire" clears the way for new growth.

Because people and emotions are involved in these situations—not just factories and office buildings—the best leaders help downsized employees build a bridge. During one reorganization with which I was involved, I was able to place some of the people that were being laid off from my area, because I had developed strong connections with business leaders both within NCR and at other organizations. I was able to ask these other leaders if they had areas of opportunity open for my soon-to-be-former employees.

WEEDING

If you have done all that you know is appropriate to help an employee become a contributing member of a team and still there are no positive results, you have to make the decision that is in the best interest of your team, the organization, and ultimately the employee.

> "FEED YOUR EAGLES AND STARVE YOUR TURKEYS."

"Feed your eagles and starve your turkeys." This is one concept that remained with Susan Sobbott since business school. The professor who said it reminded students that if you continually try to feed your turkeys, you will starve your eagles. You have to reach a point where you realize that it is more important to nurture your eagles, because no matter how hard you try, your turkeys will always be turkeys. They simply are not going to take flight. Leaders must concentrate on their star performers. Once an employee has been identified as a weed—someone who is not going to grow in the desired manner—the leader must develop a plan to tackle the problem.

Weeding is the toughest, most backbreaking part of being a gardener. It is the part of gardening that everyone dislikes. In business, "weeding" people is just as agonizing. As with weeds in the garden, some weeds in business can grow strong roots if left in place long enough. Some, like chickweed, pardon the pun, wind their way through your organization. Then there is that one that hides behind your prize flowers and is incredibly difficult to reach. It has "stickers" and pricks your fingers every time you try to remove it. Because its roots are intertwined with those of your flowers, you know you might uproot something you like when removing the weed. For this reason you continue to lop off the top of the weed, hoping it will stop growing. That rarely seems to work. No matter what the type, the longer weeds are allowed to inhabit your garden and your business, the more of a problem they become. Although maintenance can be especially difficult, at the end of the day, looking over a weed-free garden or business is incredibly satisfying.

Years ago, I took over a department that included a department manager who resented having to report to me. She was a former peer and believed she should have had my job. Within a few days of the transition, she started resisting the requirements I outlined for all the managers reporting to me. She was openly vocal in her disagreements with me and operated in a hostile manner. I had several conversations with her about her attitude, but when it became clear that this would not evolve into a mutually beneficial relationship, I recommended that she consider other opportunities within the organization. She agreed. With my assistance, she transferred to another area where she was able to contribute her best efforts. Within less than a year, she took a position with a different company. The rest of our team expressed their appreciation for my dealing with the issue quickly. It was causing a very disruptive and negative environment for everyone. I was also then able to devote more of my time to the positive aspects of the team.

Another problem with weeds is that some of them look like desirable plants. It takes a very astute and knowledgeable gardener to recognize what is or is not a weed. A friend shared a story about spending the day in the garden weeding. It was a hot day and she was incredibly exhausted. Rather than watering the garden herself, she asked her husband to do it while she took a break. After a few minutes of enjoying the air-conditioning and a cool iced tea, she looked outside to see how her husband was progressing. He was watering the bucket she had put some of the taller weeds in. He thought they were plants waiting to go in the ground. I remember very distinctly being very proud of a flower that I was cultivating in an area of my garden. It was quite a shock when a more knowledgeable gardener pointed out that I was in fact cultivating a giant weed. Even though it looked quite attractive (in fact I called my weed "weedus maximus"), it had to be removed because the plants

> "ANOTHER PROBLEM WITH WEEDS IS THAT SOME OF THEM LOOK LIKE DESIRABLE PLANTS."

around it were being choked by the weed's roots.

When I was at NCR, I remember mistaking one weed in particular for a flower. The result caused damage that took some time and a major effort on my part to straighten out. I had hired a person who on the surface seemed to be a truly motivated, supportive manager. At all of our meetings, she contributed many great and creative ideas and indicated how well her team was accomplishing their required assignments and that all timelines were on target. Unfortunately, this was not the truth.

This manager was actually telling her staff that she did not support the required work and that she was sorry to have to ask them to take on certain projects and timelines. Her team was working very long hours on projects and being told that I was aware of their problems. Fortunately, one of those employees took a risk and shared his concerns about this situation with another manager. That manager advised the employee's manager to come to me and share her problems, and assured her that if I knew the problems I would help her resolve them. Although she agreed to speak with me, she never did. I learned about this only later, when a major project was impacted negatively by the lack of support by this manager for her team. I had a conversation with the manager about her deception and failure to comply with my request. I had to put her on a warning notice with the caveat that her performance and reporting process had to change or she would be asked to leave. She left within two weeks and I had to repair the damage done to her team.

At Avon, Jill Kanin-Lovers said that they are "very clear about unacceptable behaviors and performance, which makes it easier for the organization to understand why a high-profile executive has been terminated." Although I had been clear about acceptable and unacceptable behaviors, I was not aware of some of this employee's behaviors.

Her team had been under the assumption that I knew about their problems and still did nothing to try to correct them. It took time for that team to regain their status as high performers. I also had to talk with the manager who had advised his fellow manager to speak with me. He was under the misconception that she had spoken with me and that I had chosen to do nothing. No matter how an employee leaves, it is important for the organization to maintain "face." In Chapter 2, Jill described the leadership style of Andrea Jung, CEO of Avon. Jill said that the last component of Andrea's style for making the tough decisions about people is that "the departing executive is always treated with respect and dignity. We have found this is critical, not just for the departing executive but for those remaining." There is often a feeling of "survival guilt" for employees who remain after others have been terminated or downsized. Leaders must take care to consider the emotions of the remaining employees.

One of the most demotivating factors that a leader will face if they do not address issues caused by the weeds in the department is the reaction of the employees who are meeting or exceeding job requirements. They will very quickly become resentful and most definitely not want to produce unless they see management addressing the issues caused by the weed. Leaders must address this type of issue quickly and it must be clear to the rest of the department that the issue has been addressed. They need to see that the nonperformer is being given every opportunity to address any issues they have, but they also need to know that the nonperformer is being held accountable for their actions.

Michele Coleman Mayes recounted an experience with a "very bright young woman who hit a wall." Although Michele had worked with her to answer the question about why this had occurred, it reached a point where Michele advised her it was time to move on. It is important that an employee clearly understands the ramifications of not taking the steps that are required of them. It is important that it be understood by the employee that if they are given 60 days to improve performance, they must improve. If there is no change in behavior and output, they have to understand the consequences. However, as with downsizings, it is important for the employer to provide a smooth transition. The young woman that Michele worked with had never failed at any previous job, so it was hard for her to accept what had happened. "I continued to impress upon her that there was life after Colgate," said Michele. "She left and proceeded to do well in her next position. She also recommended Colgate as a good place to work to other people. In reflection, she did not let her experience taint her overall opinion of the company. I have remained in contact with her for well over seven years." As Karen Nemetz Duvall said, "It's possible to be tough on performance and soft on people."

SUMMARY

Leaders must foster the ongoing development of others in order to achieve individual and organizational growth and success through:

- Clarity relating to expectations and performance issues
- Employee-driven solution development for performance issues
- Follow up meetings with employees to monitor progress
- Continuous and effective communication
- Recognition
- Corrective action when needed

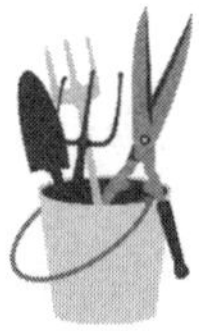

LEADERSHIP INVENTORY

1. Do you recognize and value the importance of addressing performance issues, such as setting clear corrective-action requirements, with timelines and measurements for yourself and others?

What actions have you taken to identify these issues?

How has this contributed to your growth and development?

How has this contributed to the growth and development of others?

How has this contributed to your organization's success?

What resources/activities help you to identify these issues?

When was the last time you used these resources/activities to identify issues?

2. Do you recognize and value the importance of holding employees accountable for addressing performance issues and meeting the agreed corrective-action requirements, while monitoring those actions and taking decisive appropriate action (including a warning notice, temporary suspension, or termination)?

What actions have you taken that contributed to your success in this area?

How has this contributed to your growth and development?

How has this contributed to the growth and development of others?

How has this contributed to your organization's success?

What resources/activities help you to pursue this goal?

When was the last time you used these resources/activities to pursue this goal?

3. Do you provide support to achieve corrective action and give appropriate recognition when the requirements are met?

What actions have you taken that contributed to your success in this area?

How has this contributed to your growth and development?

How has this contributed to the growth and development of others?

How has this contributed to your organization's success?

What resources/activities help you to pursue this goal?

When was the last time you used these resources/activities to pursue this goal?

CALL TO ACTION

Based upon your response to the Leadership Inventory, identify three (3) actions to further your continuing development and success as a leader.

Action	Timetable
1.	
2.	
3.	

CLOSING "THOTTES"

"BEST IN SHOW"

CLOSING "THOTTES"

"BEST IN SHOW"

I love the last line of Bette Midler's song "The Rose":

> *"Just remember in the winter, far beneath the bitter snows,*
>
> *lies the seed, that with the sun's love, in the spring,*
>
> *becomes the Rose."*

Through effective leadership, almost every person can become a rose. It takes vision, assessment, the right environment, nurturing and support, and, when needed, pruning, or weeding. If you cultivate leadership excellence, your garden will be magnificent!

When gardeners are able to enjoy those wonderful moments when their hard work results in beautiful gardens, there is one additional step to take. As Carrie Fisher said, "There is no point at which you can say, 'Well, I'm successful now. I might as well take a nap.'"

Leaders must focus on the continuing development of their leadership skills and of their star performers. In terms of skills, leaders must assess and identify those skills that have proven the most useful and maintain those from year to year. Just as the garden changes from season to season, so does the business world. Old models of leadership such as those discussed in Chapter 1 are no longer effective. In order to move forward, the leader must recognize new leadership practices, choose the most effective skills for those practices, sharpen them when they become dull, and toss them when they are no longer effective.

In business, leaders continue to develop their star performers by choosing them for "blue ribbon" acknowledgement. *Changing the Corporate Landscape* emphasizes the need to provide opportunities for employees to grow and develop. It's very important for leaders to look for opportunities outside their own departments to give star performers the opportunity to advance. Oftentimes leaders become reliant on these perennials—those employees who do such a wonderful job that their managers are loathe to let them go. Similarly, in gardening, it is difficult for gardeners to remove potential prizewinners from their gardens. However, in taking the plant to the next level—a garden show—others have the opportunity to see its beauty. That, of course, is my final point about leadership.

Helping the employee advance benefits the employee and the company. Ultimately, it also benefits the leader because the leader is seen throughout the organization as a great people-developer. Respect for the leader and his or her employee is reinforced when the employee becomes a success.

Blue-ribbon employees also add an additional benefit. As with gardening, business is cyclical. Leaders who cultivate blue-ribbon employees, cultivate future leaders. These future leaders often return to those who helped them—as important strategic alliances, friends, and possibly future clients. Although leaders each cultivate their own garden, in the big picture, we each have a patch of earth similar to what I had as a child. What we cultivate touches the gardens around us. If the garden is one that is recognized as a continual prizewinner, other gardeners take notice and are inspired to use that garden and its gardener as their own model to achieve success.

Just as every great gardener knows, and as my friend Val shared in Chapter 1, "Gardening isn't something you do once and then sit back." Leaders take the time to enjoy the beauty of the "garden" they have created and also to reflect on what they learned in the process, because they need to start thinking and preparing for the next "planting season." In order for the cycle of leadership excellence to continue, it is important that leaders always:

- Identify the workplace trends and issues
- Create a shared vision to achieve both individual and organizational goals
- Assess their leadership strengths and opportunities for improvement
- Develop an individual development plan to leverage those strengths and improve in areas of opportunity for growth

- Assess, establish, and support an environment conducive to their continued growth and success, as well as for others' and the organization's
- Establish and maintain an open, honest, and effective two-way communication process
- Provide appropriate recognition and rewards for those with whom they work
- Provide ongoing support to assist those with whom they work to achieve their full potential
- Identify those employees who may need to be transplanted or removed to ensure their continued success and the success of the organization
- Identify and provide ongoing opportunities for those star performers with whom they work

I leave you with a poem that has been one of my favorites since I was a child, and one final request. It's one we make of all our WUI graduates. As you finish this book, take a moment and reflect on what you have read and make a commitment to (1) your ongoing growth and development, and (2) the ongoing growth and development of others. May you bloom and grow forever.

Wishing you continued
growth & success!
Jean M Otte

My Commitment

Identify below at least three things you promise to do that will contribute to your ongoing growth and development:

Action Timeline

1.

2.

3.

Identify below at least three things you promise to do that will contribute to others' ongoing growth and development:

Action Timeline

1.

2.

3.

THE GLORY OF THE GARDEN

BY RUDYARD KIPLING

Our England is a garden that is full of stately views,
Of borders, beds and shrubberies and lawns and avenues,
With statues on the terraces and peacocks strutting by;
But the Glory of the Garden lies in more than meets the eye.
For where the old thick laurels grow, along the thin red wall,
You'll find the tool- and potting-sheds which are the heart of all;
The cold-frames and the hot-houses, the dung-pits and the tanks,
The rollers, carts, and drain-pipes, with the barrows and the planks.

And there you'll see the gardeners, the men and 'prentice boys
Told off to do as they are bid and do it without noise;
For, except when seeds are planted and we shout to scare the birds,
The Glory of the Garden it abideth not in words.
And some can pot begonias and some can bud a rose,
And some are hardly fit to trust with anything that grows;
But they can roll and trim the lawns and sift the sand and loam,
For the Glory of the Garden occupieth all who come.

Our England is a garden, and such gardens are not made

By singing: "Oh, how beautiful," and sitting in the shade,
While better men than we go out and start their working lives
At grubbing weeds from gravel-paths with broken dinner-knives.
There's not a pair of legs so thin, there's not a head so thick,
There's not a hand so weak and white, nor yet a heart so sick,
But it can find some needful job that's crying to be done,
For the Glory of the Garden glorifieth every one.

Then seek your job with thankfulness and work till further orders,
If it's only netting strawberries or killing slugs on borders;
And when your back stops aching and your hands begin to harden,
You will find yourself a partner in the Glory of the Garden.
Oh, Adam was a gardener, and God who made him sees
That half a proper gardener's work is done upon his knees,
So when your work is finished, you can wash your hands and pray
For the Glory of the Garden, that it may not pass away!

And the Glory of the Garden it shall never pass away!

WOMEN UNLIMITED INC.

RECOMMENDED READING LIST

(Suggestions from participants, mentors, and speakers)

CHANGE MANAGEMENT

Bridges, William. *Managing Transitions: Making the Most of Change,* 2nd ed. New York: Da Capo, 2003.
———*JobShift: How to Prosper in a Workplace Without Jobs.* New York: Da Capo, 1995.

Duck, Jeanie Daniel. "Managing Change: The Art of Balancing." *Harvard Business Review:* November 2000.

Kinsey Goman, Carol. *This Isn't the Company I Joined: Seven Steps to Energizing a Restructured Work Force.* New York: John Wiley & Sons, 1997.

Johnson, Spencer, M.D. *Who Moved My Cheese? An Amazing Way to Deal with Change in Your Work and in Your Life.* New York: G.P. Putnam's Sons, 1998.

Pritchett, Price, and Ron Pound. *Business as Unusual: The Handbook for Managing and Supervising Organizational Change,* 2nd ed. Dallas: Pritchett Publishing Company, 1994.

Tomasko, Robert M. *Rethinking the Corporation: The Architecture of Change.* New York: AMACOM, 1993.

COMMUNICATION/MANAGING RELATIONSHIPS

Deep, Sam, and Lyle Sussman. *What to Ask When You Don't Know What to Say: 555 Powerful Questions to Use for Getting Your Way at Work.* Paramus, NJ: Prentice Hall Press, 1993.

Graham Scott, Gini. *Work with Me!* Palo Alto, CA: Davies-Black Publishing, 2000.

Gray, John. *Men Are from Mars, Women Are from Venus: A Practical Guide for Improving Communication and Getting What You Want in Your Relationships.* New York: HarperCollins Publishers, 1993.

Heim, Pat, Ph.D. *Hardball for Women: Winning at the Game of Business.* New York: Plume, 1993.
———*In the Company of Women: Turning Workplace Conflict into Powerful Alliances.* New York: J.P. Tarcher, 2001.

Mendell, Adrienne. *How Men Think.* New York: Ballantine Books, 1996.

Steil, Dr. Lyman K., and Dr. Richard K. Bommelje. *Listening Leaders: The 10 Golden Rules to Listen, Lead & Succeed.* Edina, MN: Beaver's Pond Press, 2004.

Tannen, Deborah. *You Just Don't Understand: Women and Men in Conversation.* New York: William Morrow, 1990.
———*That's Not What I Meant.* New York: William Morrow, 1986.
———*Talking From 9 to 5: How Women's and Men's Conversational Styles Affect Who Gets Heard, Who Gets Credit, and What Gets Done at Work.* New York: William Morrow, 1994.

White, Kate. *Why Good Girls Don't Get Ahead but Gutsy Girls Do: Nine Secrets Every Career Woman Must Know.* New York: Warner Books, 1995.

GLASS CEILING

Catalyst Research Group. *Advancing Women in Business—The Catalyst Guide: Best Practices from the Corporate Leaders.* San Francisco: Jossey-Bass, 1998.

Conley, Frances K., M.D. *Walking Out on the Boys.* New York: Farrar, Straus and Giroux, 2000.

Griffiths, Sian, and Helena Kennedy. *Beyond the Glass Ceiling: Forty Women Whose Ideas Shape the Modern World.* Manchester, England: Manchester University Press, 1996.

Nichols, Nancy A. *Reach for the Top: Women and the Changing Facts of Work Life.* Boston: Harvard Business School Press, 1994.

GOAL SETTING/PERSONAL GROWTH

Bancroft, Nancy H. *The Feminine Quest for Success: How to Prosper in Business and Be True to Yourself.* San Francisco: Berrett-Koehler Publishers, 1995.

Covey, Stephen R. *The 7 Habits of Highly Effective People: Powerful Lessons in Personal Change.* New York: Fireside Publishers, 1990.

Estés, Clarissa Pinkola, Ph.D. *Women Who Run with the Wolves: Myths and Stories of the Wild Woman Archetype.* Reprinted, New York: Ballantine Books, 2003.

Kabat-Zinn, Jon. *Wherever You Go, There You Are.* New York: Hyperion, 1995.

WOMEN AND LEADERSHIP

Agonito, Rosemary, Ph.D. *No More "Nice Girl": Power, Sexuality and Success in the Workplace.* Avon, MA: Adams Media Corp. 1993.

Bancroft, Nancy H. *The Feminine Quest for Success: How to Prosper in Business and Be True to Yourself.* San Francisco: Berrett-Koehler Pub., 1995.

Brooks, Donna, and Lynn Brooks. *Seven Secrets of Successful Women.* New York: McGraw-Hill, 1999.

Ellig, Janice Reals and William J. Morin. *What Every Successful Women Knows: 12 Breakthrough Strategies to Get the Power and Ignite Your Career.* New York: McGraw-Hill, 2001.

Enkelis, Liane, and Karen Olsen. *On Our Terms: Portraits of Women Business Leaders.* San Francisco: Berrett-Koehler Pub., 1995.

Evans, Gail. *Play Like a Man, Win Like a Woman: What Men Know About Success That Women Need to Learn.* New York: Broadway Books, 2000.
———*She Wins, You Win: The Most Important Rule Every Businesswoman Needs to Know.* New York: Gotham Books, 2003.

Gallagher, Carol Ph.D., and Susan K. Golant. *Going to the Top: A Road Map for Success from America's Leading Women Executives.* New York: Viking, 2000.

Glaser, Connie, and Barbara Steinberg Smalley. *Swim with the Dolphins: How Women Can Succeed in Corporate America on Their Own Terms.* New York: Warner Books, 1995.

Hartman, Mary S., ed. *Talking Leadership: Conversations with Powerful Women.* Piscataway, NJ: Rutgers University Press, 1999.

Heim, Pat, and Susan K. Golant. *Hardball for Women: Winning at the Game of Business.* New York: Plume, 1993.

Kouzes, James M., with Barry Z. Posner. *Credibility: How Leaders Gain and Lose It, Why People Demand It.* San Francisco: Jossey-Bass, 1993.

McCorduck, Pamela, and Nancy Ramsey. *The Futures of Women: Scenarios for the 21st Century.* New York: Perseus, 1996.

McKenzie, Vashti M. *Strength in the Struggle: Leadership Development for Women.* Pilgrim Press, 2001.

Nichols, Nancy A., ed. *Reach for the Top: Women and the Changing Facts of Work Life.* Boston: Harvard Business School Press, 1994.

Rosener, Judy B. *America's Competitive Secret: Utilizing Women as a Management Strategy.* New York: Oxford University Press, 1995.

Shirley, Donna. *Managing Martians.* New York: Broadway Books, 1998.

White, Kate. *Why Good Girls Don't Get Ahead but Gutsy Girls Do.* New York: Warner Books, 1996.

MENTORS/MENTORING

Brounstein, Marty. *Coaching & Mentoring for Dummies.* Foster City, CA: IDG Books, 2000.

Shea, Gordon. *Mentoring: Helping Employees Reach Their Full Potential.* New York: AMACOM, 1994.

Sinetar, Marsha. *The Mentor's Spirit: Life Lessons on Leadership and the Art of Encouragement.* New York: St. Martin's Griffin, 1998.

Wellington, Sheila, and Betty Spence. *Be Your Own Mentor: Strategies from Top Women on the Secrets of Success.* New York: Random House, 2001.

Wicks, Robert J. *Sharing Wisdom: The Practical Art of Giving and Receiving Mentoring.* New York: Crossroad General Interest, 2000.

NEGOTIATION SKILLS

Fisher, Roger, William Ury, and Bruce Patton. *Getting to Yes: Negotiating Agreement Without Giving In,* 2nd ed. New York: Houghton Mifflin, 1992.

Miller, Lee E., and Jessica Miller. *A Woman's Guide to Successful Negotiating: How to Convince, Collaborate, & Create Your Way to Agreement.* New York: McGraw-Hill, 2002.

Ury, William. *Getting Past No: Negotiating Your Way from Confrontation to Cooperation,* revised ed. New York: Bantam Books, 1993.

Whitaker, Leslie, and Elizabeth Austin. *The Good Girl's Guide to Negotiating: How to Get What You Want at the Bargaining Table.* Boston: Little Brown & Company, 2001.

NETWORKING SKILLS

Mackay, Harvey. *Dig Your Well Before You're Thirsty: The Only Networking Book You'll Ever Need.* New York: Currency, 1997.

Catalyst. *Creating Women's Networks: A How-to Guide for Women and Companies.* San Francisco: Jossey-Bass, 1998.

POLITICAL SAVVY

Casperson, Dana May. *Power Etiquette: What You Don't Know Can Kill Your Career.* New York: AMACOM, 1999.

Lichtenberg, Ronna. *Work Would Be Great If It Weren't for the People.* New York: Hyperion, 1998.

Rozakis, Laurie, and Bob Rozakis. *The Complete Idiot's Guide to Office Politics.* Alpha Books, 1998.

STRESS MANAGEMENT

Eliot, Robert S., M.D. *From Stress to Strength: How to Lighten Your Load and Save Your Life.* New York: Bantam Books, 1994.

Miller, Lyle H., and Alma Dell Smith. *The Stress Solution: An Action Plan to Manage the Stress in Your Life.* New York: Pocket Books, 1993.

Witkin, Georgia, Ph.D. *The Female Stress Syndrome,* 3rd ed. New York: New Market Press, 2000.

TEAMS

Blanchard, Kenneth, Donald Carew, and Eunice Parisi-Carew. *The One Minute Manager Builds High Performing Teams.* New York:William Morrow and Company, 1991.

Hitchcock, Darcy E., and Marsha L. Willard. *Why Teams Can Fail and What to Do About It.* New York: McGraw-Hill, 1995.

Katzenbach, Jon R., and Douglas K. Smith. *The Wisdom of Teams: Creating the High-Performance Organization.* Boston: Harvard Business School Press, 1993.

TIME MANAGEMENT AND BALANCE

Apter, Terri. *Working Women Don't Have Wives: Professional Success in the 1990s.* New York: St. Martin's Press, 1994.

Booher, Dianna. *Get a Life Without Sacrificing Your Career.* New York: McGraw-Hill, 1999.

Brown, Genevieve, Beverly I. Irby, eds. *Women and Leadership: Creating Balance in Life.* Hauppauge, NY: Nova Science Publishers,1998.

Carlson, Richard, Ph.D. *Don't Sweat the Small Stuff at Work.* New York: Hyperion, 1998.
———*Don't Sweat the Small Stuff . . . and It's All Small Stuff.* New York: Hyperion, 1997.

Hochschild, Arlie. *The Time Bind: When Work Becomes Home and Home Becomes Work.* New York: Henry Holt & Company, 1997.

McGee-Cooper, Ann. *Time Management for Unmanageable People.* New York: Bantam Books, 1994.

Monaghan, Patricia. *Working Wisdom.* New York: HarperCollins, 1994.

Nicholaus, Bret, and Paul Lowrie. *The Check Book: 200 Ways to Balance Your Life.* Novato, CA: New World Library, 1999.

Sawi, Beth. *Coming Up for Air: How to Build a Balanced Life in a Workaholic World.* New York: Hyperion, 2000.

Smith, Hyrum W. *The 10 Natural Laws of Successful Time and Life Management.* New York: Warner Books, 1994.

Swiss, Deborah J., and Judith P. Walker. *Women and the Work/Family Dilemma.* New York: John Wiley and Sons, 1994.